WILLIAM SHAKESPEARE:
WRITING FOR PERFORMANCE

Also by John Russell Brown

SHAKESPEARE AND HIS COMEDIES
THEATRE LANGUAGE
DISCOVERING SHAKESPEARE
OXFORD ILLUSTRATED HISTORY OF THEATRE (*editor*)

William Shakespeare: Writing for Performance

John Russell Brown

First published 1996 by
MACMILLAN PRESS LTD
Houndmills, Basingstoke, Hampshire RG21 6XS
and London
Companies and representatives
throughout the world

ISBN 0–333–63921–9 hardcover
ISBN 0–333–63922–7 paperback

A catalogue record for this book is available
from the British Library.

10   9   8   7   6   5   4   3   2   1
05 04 03 02 01 00 99 98 97 96

Printed in Malaysia

Contents

Contents

Introduction

This book asks fundamental questions about Shakespeare and his plays. How did he work as a writer? Did he indicate, by any recoverable means, the manner in which his plays should be staged and performed? How should we respond to them as we read? Does the fact that Shakespeare wrote his plays for performance dictate the ways in which we should study them: are there right and wrong ways of thinking about his characters, the 'meaning' of the plays, or the effect and relevance of a single speech? Such questions arise naturally enough, but most books about Shakespeare do no more than glance at them while considering problems of interpretation or restoration, trying to find what use we can make of the texts or what validity they had for their original audiences. So much in Shakespeare's texts is immediately accessible to any reader, seeming to bring the speeches and characters alive in the imagination, that it is all too easy to suppose that we are in possession of the plays and are reading them appropriately. But plays written for performance are very different texts from those written for readers with a printed book in their hands: they demand a special kind of attention.

The need for theatrically conscious reading is widely acknowledged, but what exactly is this and by what means can it be achieved? Live performance before a live audience during a consecutive period of time is not easily re-created in the mind of a reader or critic, and yet this is the very element in which Shakespeare's plays were intended to exist and to reveal their distinctive natures. In other circumstances, their words are bound to be misunderstood and their dialogue, structure, spectacle, characters, argument or theme distorted. None of these features should be considered except as part of a complicated, uncertain, idiosyncratic, and ever-changing theatre performance.

A playscript is written so that it will work for the actors of a company and hold an audience's attention. Very literally it comes alive on stage (and then in the minds of an audience) by means of what the actors do, their thinking, feeling, looking, their physical actions and reactions, their breathing, intelligences, and individual imaginations, their very beings. All this belongs with the words set down in the text and greatly modifies their effect. Groupings of figures, movements across a stage, and sounds which echo around a theatre and seem to hang in its air, are also added to the words. A play has to be seen and heard in order to be understood. We must also recognise that an audience will respond in unpredictable ways, and that too will affect the playing of a text. It seems impossible for a reader to compensate for the loss of all this, but these factors are more than usually relevant for Shakespeare. His plays are so thoroughly geared to the demands of performance that they have been sought out by theatres around the world, representing many different cultures and traditions of performance. His plays, above all plays, deserve to be read and judged theatrically.

This book does not debate the rights and wrongs of any interpretation of a play or argue about the physical details and standard practices of the playhouses of Shakespeare's day. It makes no assessment of his view of the world. Such questions are touched upon, but the main concern is to ask how writing for performance governed what Shakespeare wrote and how this can be taken into account when reading the plays.

Understanding the theatrical element of the plays is not so difficult as it would have been some years ago, because the nature of live performance has become the subject of intensive study by theatre historians and theoreticians. Besides, those who write plays today or help to stage them in our theatres have become more helpful to critics by making their experiences much more available than before in interviews, public workshops, and biographical and technical writings. A very great deal is known now about the demands of performance which this book can bring to the study of Shakespeare's texts, and there is no longer any reason why literary criticism should be cordoned off from theatrical practicalities and uncertainties.

It would have been possible to begin with a careful dissection of the elements of any theatrical experience and then look for signs in the texts of what Shakespeare's words require from actors and from theatrically aware readers. But the study of performance in general uses technical terms which are not yet widely known or defined to everyone's satisfaction and so, rather than starting with explanations of these and establishing Shakespeare's difference from other writers, I have throughout taken the terms which arise from a study of Shakespeare's texts and used them to develop a way of talking about theatrical performance. By following the clues implicit in a wide sampling of incidents in the plays, I have tried to uncover Shakespeare's particular sense of what is involved in performance. From there I move on to consider the shaping of whole plays.

Having few obvious predecessors, this book is frequently elementary and exploratory. Numerous stage histories of individual plays have been published and notable Shakespearian performances have been annotated and criticised in great detail, but these studies contain little direct help in the present enquiry; they say rather more about actors and directors than they do about intrinsic qualities in the writing. Shakespeare's ideas of theatre and his characteristic dramatic techniques are still such open questions that raising them offers new opportunities for study and critical engagement with the plays.

In the last sixty or so years, archaeological and documentary research and a methodical sifting of textual evidence gathered from all the existing plays of the period have together furnished a more accurate picture of Elizabethan theatres than was possessed earlier, and a clearer idea of how production was managed. We also know more about Shakespeare's audiences and about the many references to contemporary life and ideas in his plays and other writings of the time. These studies lie behind the writing of this book, even though it does not take direct notice of the various scholarly debates which are now in progress. Sometimes it takes sides in these issues, but without entering fully into the reasons why each choice has been made; such arguments would have taken too much space and obscured the main exposition. The same is true of the many books about acting which have been published since the end of the nineteenth century, both those giving advice to modern actors and those seeking to uncover attitudes to the art which were current in Shakespeare's day. But on the other hand, throughout the book some time has been taken to consider what modern dramatists have said about writing for performance and to listen to what some of our finest actors have said about their performances; these practitioners are in a position to take us closer to an understanding of Shakespeare's craftsmanship than anyone who has not worked in a theatre.

Another feature of this book calls for some explanation and defence. While its first chapter tries to place Shakespeare in the

theatre of his own time, in contrast to late twentieth-century buildings and theatre-practice, this historical setting becomes less dominant as the book's argument develops. The phraseology and
emphasis introduced in the opening chapter influence all the argument, but when considering practicalities of staging the usual
reference is not to a reconstruction of an 'Elizabethan' theatre or
theatres, but to the very basic notion of a performance taking
place on a platform stage surrounded on three sides by an audience, with that audience sitting and standing in the same light as
the actors. Similarly for acting, reference is to actors performing
with little rehearsal, speaking the words provided, giving individual physical and mental presence to each speaker and hearer,
and maintaining interaction with each other and with their audience. These are, I believe, the most significant circumstances that
defined theatre-practice in Shakespeare's day.

Nothing can eliminate a certain dependence in this book on
conjecture and hypothesis. Keeping close to Shakespeare's own
words for describing performance has been the main check upon
misrepresentation and misjudgement, but I have also used two
further safeguards. The more important is my experience, at London's National Theatre and elsewhere, of seeing many plays come
alive during rehearsals in very simple and open conditions. Almost as useful has been travel around the world to see plays and
other events in conditions far closer to the Elizabethan than any
to be found in most Western theatres which produce Shakespeare
today.[1] Both these practical advantages have alerted me to
aspects of Shakespeare's stagecraft that I would not have seen
otherwise and given me some insight into the behaviour of his
audiences.

*   *   *

All quotations from Shakespeare follow the *Complete Works*,
edited by Peter Alexander (London: Collins, 1951), except for some
small changes of punctuation and the omission of some stage
directions.

1
Theatre

When contemporary playwrights are asked what it is like to work in theatre, every one answers differently. Edward Bond talks about challenging the actors:

> In a lot of modern theatre writing, what is important is the throwing back of the line to each other, like playing tennis, whereas my dialogue is like tennis players playing billiards. They have that sort of rapport, but they also have to have this plotting and scheming.[1]

This was in 1975, and soon afterwards Bond was saying that his task was to create a new kind of theatre. This 'rational theatre' would be in opposition to the facile and spineless ones is evidence elsewhere:

> Theatre, when it's doing what it was created to do, demonstrates order in chaos, the ideal in the ordinary, history in the present, the rational in the seemingly irrational.[2]

For Howard Brenton, the task is to be bold and striking, so that other people pay attention:

> If a play is really going to work, it is going to be an event in public – as much an event as a car crash or the sudden death of the Prime Minister in strange circumstances. . . . But the point about theatre is that it's consciously done, it's thought out, it's rigged if you like. . . . I would very much like to change the world with my plays. I know it's a ludicrous ambition, but nevertheless it is an ambition.[3]

In contrast, back in 1959, John Osborne was ebullient and confident:

I think anything that makes the theatre alive and vital is good for it – and I don't think it ever has been as vital or alive as it is now. If people are moved to walk out, or to yell out rude things, it shows they're responding – they're not just sitting there. I think it's splendid.[4]

These three are all set on getting a response from their audience, gripping them and changing them. But other playwrights in the same British theatre see their task quite differently. Alan Ayckbourn does not look far beyond the play in hand:

I feel a bit like I'm standing on a rickety staircase – I suppose I ought to get it mended, but if I did, I might lose a lot of material, so I continue to sway to and fro nervously on top. I don't think perfect people can write plays very easily; I think the more flaws the better, which is why writers are often such extraordinarily anti-social and difficult people to talk to.[5]

Tom Stoppard, speaking about his job during a busy time, put it like this:

I got the image [for it] the other day. . . . You know, those Chinese acrobat people who spin plates – they have twenty plates spinning and every time one's about to wobble and fall off, they have to run and give them another wobble. I've got four plates spinning.[6]

For David Mamet the task of writing plays is a search for something solid and firm:

. . . when he does talk about writing, he is likely to grab hold of a hand-made chair in his kitchen and liken himself to its maker. He loves writing in part because it involves producing something tangible, something he can hold and read and ultimately see on the stage.[7]

How would Shakespeare have described what it was like to be a writer for the theatre? If we *knew* – if he had been interviewed, as celebrities are constantly interviewed and recorded today – we might learn how his mind worked and how to read and stage his plays rather better. What he said might have been something less than the truth – interviews catch only opinions of the moment – but his choice of image and emphasis would have revealed something about the bias of his mind which is hard to learn by other means. It would not *explain* anything, but might help us to recognise the strategies underlying the writing and to appreciate some of the forces at work in his mind as he wrote. Present-day dramatists reveal something of their distinctive styles in this way.

Some dramatists contemporary with Shakespeare did find ways of telling their audiences and readers what they thought about their art. Ben Jonson introduced characters to expound critical opinions and speak for their author. He also wrote *Timber: or Discoveries made upon Men and Matter*, which was published posthumously; it is indebted to Latin authors, but includes instruction, based on Jonson's own experience, on how to write plays. He also had his say about the worth of a number of contemporary writers. Occasionally other dramatists wrote a preface, dedication, prologue or extended note for an edition of a play in which they expressed critical opinions or explained their reason for writing or publishing. A very few wrote pamphlets or other prose works which contain comments on the art of a dramatist. It is not surprising to find sophisticated dramatists doing this, such as Jonson, John Webster or George Chapman, but equally forthcoming were more popular ones like Thomas Heywood, who wrote or had a chief hand in some two hundred plays, and Thomas Dekker, who often worked in collaboration and to order.

It was by his own choice, then, that Shakespeare has left no testimony. Nothing said in any of the plays can be quoted as his own opinion, for every line of dialogue was written to express the thoughts of a particular character in a particular situation, and only the one very small part of a (non-dramatic) Poet in *Timon of Athens* comes anywhere near to the circumstances of Shakespeare's career.

However, in the absence of any statement made 'for the record' about his art, the plays themselves do provide us with one unmistakable and positive lead on how Shakespeare thought about his work: every one of them contains moments when the theatre provided him an image for expressing a character's involvement in the play's action, or for representing his or her most private thoughts. Whatever the subject of the dialogue, Shakespeare's mind had access to the business of theatre. Actors, studying words to speak, and their gestures, actions, and roles; theatre performances, both successful and unsuccessful; audiences, theatre-buildings, stages, costumes, stage-properties: these are some of the theatrical concerns which rose to Shakespeare's mind as he wrote his plays, when neither plot nor situation had anything to do with his own profession as playwright. He drew upon his specialist theatre experience instinctively, without apology or sign of hesitation, and in many images which rise incidentally in the plays we may discover something about Shakespeare's distinctive attitudes to his art. A sharp epithet or urgent repetition can suggest the author's own involvement underlying the imagined sentiments of the character.

*   *   *

The most evocative theatrical images, which seem to jump out of the texts as if especially alive in the writer's mind, are almost all concerned with acting and audiences. A recurrent concern is for the reception of a performance:

> A jest's prosperity lies in the ear
> Of him that hears it, never in the tongue
> Of him that makes it.
> > (*Love's Labour's Lost*, V.ii.849–51)

> Life's but a walking shadow, a poor player,
> That struts and frets his hour upon the stage,
> And then is heard no more.
> > (*Macbeth*, V.v.24–6)

> You have put me now to such a part which never
> I shall discharge to th'life.
> > (*Coriolanus*, III.ii.105–6)

> . . . in a theatre, the eyes of men,
> After a well-grac'd actor leaves the stage,
> Are idly bent on him that enters next,
> Thinking his prattle to be tedious; . . .
> > (*Richard II*, V.ii.23–6)

When we are born, we cry that we are come
To this great stage of fools.

(Lear, IV.vi.183–4)

All these quotations are what Shakespeare's characters say, not the dramatist's own thoughts. They tell us about Lear's despair, Coriolanus' unease, the Duke of York's uncertainty after changing allegiance, and about Rosaline in *Love's Labour's Lost* as she holds back from reckless happiness. But they do tell us that, in order to set his characters before us, the author's own creative mind turned repeatedly towards theatrical performance.

When Shakespeare brought the players to Elsinore in *Hamlet* and so dealt directly with the business of professional theatre, he elaborated the detail at a length that the necessary business of the main play scarcely seems to warrant. The writer's personal involvement may be betrayed in various kinds of over-emphasis and in images of torrent, tempest, and whirlwind joined with those of purchase, birth, and strict control:

Speak the speech, I pray you, as I pronounc'd it to you, trippingly on the tongue. . . . Nor do not saw the air too much with your hand, thus, but use all gently; for in the very torrent, tempest, and, as I may say, whirlwind of your passion, you must acquire and beget a temperance that may give it smoothness. . . . Be not too tame neither, but let your own discretion be your tutor. (*Hamlet*, III.ii.1–17)

Leave thy damnable faces and begin.
(Hamlet, III.ii.247)

Shakespeare identified easily with actors. Ulysses in *Troilus and Cressida* is a clever and deceitful politician, but on several occasions Shakespeare gave him insights that relate to concerns other than those of the play. The task of persuading Achilles to leave his tent and fight leads him to generalise about life in terms of performance:

. . . no man is the lord of anything,
Though in and of him there be much consisting,
Till he communicate his parts to others;

> Nor doth he of himself know them for aught
> Till he behold them formed in th'applause
> Where th'are extended ...
>   (*Troilus and Cressida*, III.iii.115–20)

We might deduce from this that Shakespeare wrote plays in order to be 'Lord' of the world in which he found himself, and that
he discovered the truth about himself in the applause which greeted
their performance. That, of course, is speculation, but quite other
evidence points in the same direction. The remarkable outline of
Shakespeare's career, as deduced from legal papers, account books,
and other documentary evidence, argues for some quite exceptional drive behind his work in the theatre. We know that he
was a member of an acting company and sometimes received
moneys on its behalf; and that he was also one of a group of
'sharers' in the ownership of theatres. Moreover he was highly
successful for more than twenty very productive years and afterwards settled down to a gentleman's retirement in a large house
set in spacious gardens in the best part of his native Stratford-
upon-Avon. No other dramatist of his time achieved so much in
material rewards and, more significantly, none could equal his
almost regular tally of two plays a year over such a stretch of
time. He became a celebrity, renowned, imitated, and remarkably secure in his chosen profession. He developed those theatrical means that were at his disposal, for at a time when theatre
was a national pastime, Shakespeare worked for only one company and his fortunes rose with it so that it became hailed as the
best in the land. He used the physical resources of the playhouses
with great invention and, to judge from the experience of acting
in his plays today, he also contrived to lead his actors forward to
attempt ever more taxing parts and never to be content with repetition from play to play. He wrote for special occasions and special
audiences, as well as for the most popular of London playhouses;
and what he wrote for the general public was in demand at the
courts of both Elizabeth I and James I, and is still in demand
today.

*   *   *

The resources of the theatre within which Shakespeare worked can reveal something more about how he worked. None of our contemporary dramatists write for such a theatre. Today their careers develop far more slowly and deliberately. Those few who write as much as one stage-play a year are considered in danger of being glib and repetitive, and yet their scripts are likely to be half the length of most of Shakespeare's, and nowhere near as complex in plot or action. When modern plays are successful they run for much longer and far more consistently. Stages are provided with scenery, technical devices, lighting, sound. Productions are complex and carefully prepared and controlled. Audiences sit in the dark and assemble in the evening rather than in the middle of the day. During the twentieth century theatre has moved ever further away from the Shakespearian model, influenced by new generations of producers, technicians, designers, directors, and by economic, social, scientific and cultural changes of great magnitude.

The words which Shakespeare's contemporaries used to describe the resources and functions of theatre are, in themselves, revealing of what they thought theatre should be and indicate how far away current practice has moved. At first scholars used the terms 'inner stage', 'upper stage' and 'main stage' to describe the physical structure of Elizabethan playhouses, and they wrote of 'downstage' and 'upstage', in all this reflecting a twentieth-century notion of a three-dimensional theatrical reality viewed from one position and in one direction. In Shakespeare's day such phrases were never used; the people who worked in the Globe Theatre did not think in that way. The performers simply *'entered'* the play's action by coming *'on stage'* through a doorway, or they were *'discovered'* by drawing a curtain. Usually *'Enter'* and *'Exit'* were sufficient terms to set the action in motion, and no one was confined to any particular part of the stage. Some characters were directed to *'enter to'* others already on stage; and on leaving they were sometimes told to *'withdraw'*. On occasion an entry or exit might be through a trap door or, less frequently, by means of a chair let down from the 'heavens' over the stage, but the actors always performed 'out' on the stage, and were free to move as they wished before the audience and in relation to other actors in the play. Stage properties were *'brought out'*, *'put forth'*, or *'thrust forth'*. A character might be *'brought in sick in a chair'*,[8] serving men *'come forth'*,[9] or some soldiers *'stand forth'*.[10] A stage direction in *The Taming of the Shrew* explains that one character should enter before the others: '*Enter Biondello, Lucentio and Bianca, Gremio is out before*';[11] in *Timon of Athens* the hero's creditors are directed to '*wait for his coming out*'.[12] Shakespeare thought of his actors stepping forth onto an open space in order to 'discharge' their parts[13] and perform 'bravely'.[14]

Neither Shakespeare nor his contemporaries knew of a 'producer', 'director', 'stage-manager', 'technical director' or 'production manager'. The plays were performed without any of these controlling influences; on stage the actors were in charge of what happened, and they survived as best they could, even if the play was being performed for one night only, after a gap of several weeks, and with almost no preparatory rehearsal. The actors took possession of their author's words and then they were in charge of the play as it achieved performance on a broad, uncluttered stage, some forty by thirty feet in size. They were surrounded on three sides by an audience which shared the same light within the circle of the auditorium. Few spectators had a fixed seat allotted to them, and many of them stood to watch the performance and were free to move around in the 'yard' which surrounded the 'scaffolding' of the stage. The actors had to take charge of this audience as they gave life to the play.

When Hamlet talks about acting, he insists on a careful suiting of word to action and on the performance of a speech in imitation of the author's model pronunciation; the speech should be spoken 'trippingly on the tongue', with due temperance and smoothness, and the actor's 'discretion' must be in control. These instructions have been taken as Shakespeare's own advice to the players, but they represent only Hamlet's view of what makes good theatre: everything must be just right, and it must please one 'judicious' auditor rather than the crowded galleries and yard of the Globe. Elsewhere, when it is not an amateur playwright speaking, Shakespeare's characters all speak about acting as if what matters is that performance should be true and revealing, and that above all it should be lively and fully alive, responsive to a 'whole theatre of others' and alert to all kinds of stimulus.

Such a theatre has little to do with a director's careful placing and tuning of a twentieth-century production; it is more related to the fire and insecurity of an author's creative mind. It is interesting, but perhaps not surprising, that it is in the imagination of its dramatists that twentieth-century theatre comes closest to Shakespeare's. Then indeed performance had to be quick and skilful like a game of tennis, depending on close rapport; it was also full of 'plotting and scheming', like billiards. It was both ordered and chaotic: for the actors, it had an element of danger, like a rickety staircase or a juggling act in which too many plates are spinning. An audience might well have yelled out. When an appropriate energy did not flow between the actors on the stage, the whole engagement might have seemed utterly sterile. On the open stage there was always the possibility of unexpected discovery, as actors attempted to bring a text tangibly alive before their audience: a happening, witnessed in just this form only on this particular occasion.

The management of entries and exits, the provision of costume changes and large and small stage-properties, together with a full repertoire of off-stage sound effects and music, all required some organisation as well as adroit improvisation. Again the words used by theatre people in Shakespeare's day indicate how this job was tackled, and are quite different from those in use today. We speak of a wardrobe, wardrobe supervisor, and dressers, not of the 'tiring-house' or 'tire-house'; there is no 'tireman' or 'tiremaster', the person in an Elizabethan theatre who was in charge of the great stock of varied (and often very expensive) costumes which was needed for the daily change of repertory and who saw that they were *worn* appropriately as well as stored. He seems to have been dresser or make-up assistant as well, having on occasion, as John Marston tells us, to glue a beard on at high speed.[15] The remarkable nature of the tiremaster's job becomes clear when it is considered in practical terms. He was in charge of the costumes for up to two dozen actors appearing in some thirty different plays during a single season.

Yet he had to work in the small space that was all that could be spared in narrow and poorly lit accommodation arranged on three levels at the back of the stage. Perhaps his store spilled over to cellars under the stage or to the attics of the building, but that would not ease the tiremaster's problems during the running of a play. Shakespeare's *Coriolanus* requires at least eight costume changes for the leading man alone, and halfway through *Julius Caesar* the whole cast has to take off civilian clothes and put on military dress and armour. There is no verbal or visual evidence that leading actors had separate dressing rooms or separate dressers. A green room, to which actors could retire and keep out of other people's way, was not provided in theatres before the beginning of the eighteenth century; a visitor back-stage at the Globe was directed simply to the 'tirehouse' where the 'tiremaster' was in charge.

Some other verbal usages fall into place once we begin to visualise (and, perhaps, hear) all that was going on in the tiringhouse. The 'stage-keeper' and 'book-keeper' were the anchor-men in the complex operation – 'keeper' was the appropriate word for both functions – and they were in turn dependent on 'the book', or play-script, marked up with notes for actors and properties to be 'ready' ahead of entry cues. Alongside the racks of costumes, often bulky with the elaborate stuffing and farthingales of the period, we must also visualise a great line-up of properties, all shunted into correct positions for the sequence of scenes in each new play as the repertoire changed daily. A single important throne could take up a good deal of floor-space, and so could other practicable properties such as altars for churches, beds, bowers, tables fitted out for elaborate banquets, tombs, desks for 'studies', bars and other equipment for trial-scenes, tents, chariots, and so forth. The sheer number of some kinds of objects could be difficult to manage: bills, partisans, pikes, different kinds of swords, bucklers, rapiers, daggers; with two sizeable armies and their leaders, thirty or forty varied weapons might be needed. (Such articles would have to be accurately appropriate to each situation, for many in the audience would be expert in their use.) Other properties were awkward to handle in the confined, darkish space on three narrow floors of the tiring-house: torches that must be brought on stage blazing fiercely, red-hot fires, full jugs of ale or wine, a coffin carried on by a long and slow-moving procession to the sound of a tolling bell. Others could get lost very easily: special rings or miniatures which should be instantly recognisable, appropriate purses of money, loose coins, dishes of steaming water, phials of poison, and sundry letters and proclamations. In the last scene of *Othello*, the hero uses three different weapons, and at least one had to be secreted on stage well ahead of time, probably when the bed was '*brought forth*'. No wonder the 'stagekeeper' had a 'plot' written out, scene by scene, to help him and his actors keep some kind of order and state in all the entries and exits. No wonder a 'book-keeper' was said to 'stamp and stare (God bless us!) . . . when the actors miss their entrance'.[16]

A play had to keep its audience continuously engaged by entries from a busy, overflowing, and ill-lit tiring-house, during what

was called 'the two hours' traffic of our stage', (The Prologue to
The Two Noble Kinsmen refers to 'two hours travel' or 'travail'.) A
play lived on stage by means of a sustained, ever-fresh, and complicated activity, involving numbers of people, variously dressed
and equipped, issuing forth from back-stage and taking command
of a large empty space without hesitation, using their poet's prepared words and whatever sense of character and situation they
could bring to the creation of an illusion of life. They were surrounded by two thousand or more spectators who were free to
talk, move, eat, drink, react, or cut off attention just as they wished.
A bad actor might find some kind of reassurance by stomping
onto the stage and listening for the sound he could make 'Twixt
his stretch'd footing and the scaffoldage'.[17] This was the theatre,
in all its turmoil and uncertainty, which was in Shakespeare's
mind as he wrote his plays, the practical stage-world that must
have co-existed with whatever refinement and precision a Hamlet could imagine and with the wider visionary theatre imagined
by the chorus in *Henry V*:

> A kingdom for a stage, princes to act,
> And monarchs to behold the swelling scene!
> (Prologue, ll. 3–4)

*   *   *

One further clue to Shakespeare's idea of a play in performance
is more indirect. When a character refers to the theatre in allu-
sive terms, we may catch a glimpse, through metaphor or simile,
of the way in which theatre was related to other experiences in
Shakespeare's mind.

Such clues are most numerous in *Hamlet*, the play in which an
exceptional number of new word-usages may indicate a more than
usual excitement in composition. When Hamlet momentarily sees
himself as an actor, Shakespeare's mind ranged far and wide:

> Would not this, sir, and a forest of feathers – if the rest of my
> fortunes turn Turk with me – with two Provincial roses on my
> raz'd shoes, get me a fellowship in a cry of players, sir?
> (*Hamlet*, III.ii.269–72)

The actors are in 'fellowship', like a medieval guild and like a group of friends who stick together. (In his will Shakespeare remembered no one from London except two of his 'fellows' from the acting company, Heminges and Condell.) They are also outlandish, their fortunes on a par with those of the Turks. To join them one would need a copious 'forest of feathers'. The 'Provincial' (Provençal) rose, on each of the 'razed' shoes (elaborately slashed or, possibly, 'raised' or elevated), is the kind of rose which was reputed to have a hundred separate petals. But the most extraordinary phrase in Hamlet's speech is the 'cry of players': actors are like a pack of hounds, kept together by a huntsman, loud in cry and lusting for the chase; they are like animals, who are bred with special care, deep-breathing and sweating in pursuit, perplexed at a cold scent; and they must be restrained at the kill.

The image of the 'cry of players' suggests that actors in a theatre company have a corporate strength; and that they physically strong, specialised, energetic, instinctive, trained, and cruel. This was not the only time that Shakespeare associated actors with hunting. Earlier in this play, when Hamlet was not so impassioned, he had welcomed the 'tragedians of the city' as his friends and said he longed to see them perform: 'We'll e'en to't like French falconers, fly at anything we see' (*Hamlet*, II.ii.424–45). Here actors are hunters working together to make a kill: expert, active, swift, instinctive, and their corporate efforts air-borne and uncertain.

In an earlier play, *King John*, actors are likened to clever, skilful and diligent craftsmen, when onlookers, 'as in a theatre', are said to

> . . . gape and point
> At your *industrious* scenes and acts of death.
> (*John*, II.i.375–6)

In *Julius Caesar* the conspirators are encouraged to emulate actors in unflinching purpose and behaviour:

> . . . bear it as our Roman actors do,
> With untir'd spirits and formal constancy.
> (*Caesar*, II.i.226–7)

In the Prologue to *Henry V* and an early scene of *Macbeth*,

Shakespeare wrote of the 'swelling scene' and 'swelling act',[18] a metaphor for theatrical performance suggesting that it grows ever more complete and powerful with the energy of its own effort: proud, inflated, pregnant with hidden life. The rise of the common player to be an artist of great skill, independence, and individuality was one of the most important developments of the Elizabethan theatre,[19] but they were also 'fellows' and 'sharers', members of a company. Together they became a 'cry of players', confident, incorporated, daring, merciless.

In addition to leading actors who shone in the principal roles, others would be required to sustain the dramatic interest throughout each of Shakespeare's plays: they are all what would today be called 'company plays'. The opening scene of *Titus Andronicus* shifts from one centre of interest to another, from Saturninus to Bassianus (each with his followers), and then to Marcus. These groups are followed on stage by Titus at the centre of a long procession made up of Romans and Goths. Soon everyone turns to Tamora as she appeals for her son's life, and then her remaining sons and Titus's sons come forward and contend together. Next Lavinia makes a separate entrance and only then does Marcus take charge again; the whole crowd on stage becomes intent on electing an emperor by acclamation. Then Lavinia is abducted by her brothers, Titus kills one of his sons, and the new Emperor espouses Tamora and advances her two surviving brothers to the centre of the stage. And in all this, the silent figure of Aaron the Moor has stood apart, watching and ready to take over when the others at last leave the stage. The tragedy has opened with elaborate stage-business and continual shifts of attention; no less than thirty actors are needed to make up the opposed groups and to provide adequate force for each element in the drama. Without at least so large and disciplined a company the narrative would be muddled; and without energetic performances on all sides the drama would become only foolish. One after another, twelve distinctly individual characters are crucial for the developing action, and four of these have to be provided with a significant number of loyal followers.

From the start of his career, Shakespeare imagined his plays performed by a whole fellowship of players. The end of *Love's Labour's Lost* is a complicated dance, both in words and in contrasted groups of persons, and this is punctuated by individual contributions that break through the communal activity. Yet a single

new character, Marcade, is able to subvert the corporate movement with a brief message telling of the King's death; without a
response from each one of the characters already on stage,
Marcade's message would fail to 'cloud' the scene as the text requires. Much of the last act of *The Merchant of Venice*, after Shylock
has left the stage in Act IV, is a delicately managed game of hide-
and-seek that needs to be acted with spirit and with subtlety of
rapport. So played, the comedy can reveal unresolved antagonisms
threatening subversion, and the reconciliation of lovers can seem
a conscious act of make-believe. Without a fellowship of actors
responding with a mutually aware finesse, the end of this comedy can become trivial and over-long.

An obvious element in the early History plays is a sense of
conflict and danger as one group of characters ranges itself against
another; whole armies are suggested by the activity of twenty to
thirty actors, dressed in opposing colours. But other episodes set
in throne rooms, parliaments, or churches are no less occasions
for corporate performance. To a reader such scenes can appear
formal and long-winded, but modern productions have revealed
their inherent drama by carefully controlled grouping and costuming,
and by nice timing of statement and counterstatement. The actors
in Shakespeare's theatre, without the benefit of repeated drilling
under a director's eye, would need to be very alert and resourceful
to grip an audience in a comparable way. In their original performances these scenes of debate and argument might well have
been as full of risk and interest as the large-scale battle sequences.

Troilus and Cressida is probably the most risk-laden play of all,
for even its set debates, with numerous actors formally organ-
ised around a General or King, have hidden springs of action
and unexpected outcomes. The last scenes are especially difficult
and very expensive to stage. Each person in the drama struggles
to assert some kind of strength or find some new quarry to pur-
sue; in full cry, the players are split up and dispersed, and called
upon to follow their own instincts.

Troilus was written in the early years of the seventeenth century and it was about this time that Shakespeare stopped appearing on stage as one in the pack of actors; his membership of
the actors' company continued, but only as a 'sharer' in its business affairs and as its chief poet. Yet in his writing he continued
to rely on the actors' corporate strength in performance, his imagination creating new quarries for the hunt. While the stage is

full at the end of *Cymbeline*, the centre of this composition is occupied by an almost powerless and thoroughly mistaken king;
here it is the plot which carries the drama to its conclusion, in a
notoriously large number of contrived *dénouements*. Finally a new,
off-stage centre of interest is introduced, when a Soothsayer ex-
pounds the oracle and explains that

> The fingers of the pow'rs above do tune
> The harmony of this peace.
>
> (V.v.464–5)

Thereafter the King calls on everyone to laud the gods, as if the
contrivance of the poet, who had set the events of this complex
play in action, had been a representation of a superhuman control.

In *The Tempest*, written just before the end of his career with
Henry VIII and a number of collaborative works, Shakespeare placed
the manipulator of the play's plot on stage, in the figure of Prospero.
In the last scene, the whole cast enters, at his command, and until
this magician relinquishes power the persons of the drama are as
much at one as they could ever be, arrested in the pursuit of
their own particular quarries. This is the one play in which actors do actually appear on stage as hounds – called Fury, Silver,
Mountain and Tyrant. In *A Midsummer Night's Dream*, Shakespeare's
earlier comedy involving enchantment, the hounds had been kept
off-stage, but could have been heard as they were prepared for
the chase with huntsmen's horns.

Throughout his career Shakespeare imagined his plays being
performed by a company of actors who emerged from the crowded
and busy tiringhouse to give life to the characters he had set down
in dialogue. The 'fury', the 'quicksilver' speed, and the tyrannic
and mountainous power of their performance, both individual
and corporate, kindled his imagination as he foresaw them all in
full cry and free flight in search of the quarry which he had set
before them. Dramatic focus could become precise and intense,
action could slow down almost to a halt, and a few characters, or
only one, could hold complete attention. Besides calling up the
'untired spirits' of the whole company in the busy 'travail' of the
stage, the poet kept watch for his own purposes and, when necessary, spoke through a single person or kept the stage entirely empty
for a brief moment. He remained in charge of the hunt and followed the hounds for his own satisfaction.

*   *   *

Implied in the almost ungovernable stage-life that was brought into being through Shakespeare's imagination and the actors' performances are the two further elements of pain and discovery, both experienced by a 'cry' of hounds.

Here perhaps the words on Antonin Artaud and Jean Genet can help in expressing what was involved and which should be recreated today as we read and perform the plays. In a letter to the director of his play *The Screens*, Genet wrote:

> The actor must act quickly, even in his slowness, but his speed lightninglike, will amaze. That and his acting will make him so beautiful that, when he is snatched up by the emptiness of the wings, the audience will experience a feeling of sadness, a kind of regret: they will have seen a meteor loom into view and pass by. This kind of acting will give life to the actor and to the play. Therefore: appear, shine, and, as it were, die. . . .

> If I wanted the stage bathed in bright light, it was to keep each actor from covering up his errors, his fleeting mistakes, his fatigue, or his indifference, in a redeeming darkness. Of course, this much light will hurt him, but to be so brightly lighted will perhaps compel him.[20]

Genet was often thinking about a single exemplary actor, but when he writes about a whole cast of actors he moves closer to Shakespeare's image of the chase: 'actors . . . throw themselves into performance and emerge victorious from it'.[21] This is not a fixed and predetermined contest – for 'at first no one knows anything' – and the effect of victory is not only death but also 'discovery'.

Shakespeare did not issue manifestos or make claims for the significance of theatre, and seldom did he come close to the apocalyptic language of Artaud, but his 'cry of players' does imply the kill and the smell of blood. Translated into a different cultural and social context, that phrase belonging to an impassioned and excited Hamlet might well imply the qualities which Artaud claimed for theatre in contrast to radio and other mechanical means of communication:

And I shall henceforth devote myself
exclusively
to the theatre
as I understand it
a theatre of blood
a theatre which at every performance will have achieved
some gain

bodily,
to him who plays as well as to him who comes to see the
playing

moreover
one doesn't play
one acts.
The theatre is in reality the *genesis* of creation.
It will be done.[22]

When Shakespeare's imagination 'bodied forth' the forms of 'things
unknown', both the poet and the actors, 'with untir'd spirits and
formal constancy', were put at risk in the creation of an illusion
of reality.

2

Words

It is tempting to idealise Elizabethan actors, but Shakespeare did not. While his imagination was fed by what they might achieve, he was a writer and, in common with other dramatists, likely to be very suspicious of what could happen to his texts in performance. Judging from what his characters say about actors, their failures were as much in his mind as their successes. When Shakespeare wrote about a perfect art, it was not about theatre but poetry – about the god Orpheus singing to his lute, when music joined with words to compel attention:

> For Orpheus' lute was strung with poets' sinews,
> Whose golden touch could soften steel and stones,
> Make tigers tame, and huge leviathans
> Forsake unsounded deeps to dance on sands.
> (*Two Gentlemen of Verona*, III.ii.78–81)

The idea is found again in *Henry VIII*, at the very end of his career:

> Orpheus with his lute made trees,
> And the mountain tops that freeze,
> Bow themselves when he did sing. . . .
> (III.i.3–5)

Almost every character of significance is alive to the power of words, aware of what they can do, how they can be managed, or how they may be received. Numerous speeches, as we have seen, suggest that Shakespeare's presentation of a scene was informed by the idea of a play in performance or of a character as an actor, but in almost every scene of every play his characters speak about the use of words. Words, they say, are to be weighed, exchanged, transformed, repeated, played with, used with conscious intent,

18

dismissed as meaningless or false. Words are said to multiply and breed, disguise themselves, become wild, weak, gentle, bold, hateful, desired. They are wrestled with and wooed; they are used aptly, and misused. Words make up an unruly world and yet, at certain times, they are able to suggest a perfect and timeless existence beyond the reach of ordinary men and women. They also deceive and lie.

Statistically, at least, this serried evidence argues that words obsessed Shakespeare in a way that actors and performance did not. The persons of the plays were defined by the words he gave to them and he took obvious pleasure in this means he used. His word-hoard was enormous, and he was constantly ransacking it, adding to it, and forcing it to his purpose.

*　*　*

In his early plays, written before Shakespeare was thirty years old, words are often said to be dangerous. His characters speak of 'witching' or 'bewitching' words.[1] 'Sweet' and 'honeyed' words are not only attractive, but deceitful as well: 'By guileful fair words peace may be obtain'd.'[2] Words can poison: 'Envenom him with words, or get thee gone.' They can corrupt and be corrupted: 'This bawd, this broker, this all-changing word.'[3] Queen Margaret deceives Henry the Sixth and yet is noted for:

> ... her grace in speech,
> Her words y-clad with wisdom's majesty.
> (*2 Henry VI*, I.i.32–3)

Richard the Third declares that his 'tongue could never learn sweet smoothing word', but he knows that 'sugar'd words' can hide 'poison' in the hearts of enemies and he uses 'honey words' to make captive a 'woman's heart'.[4] The 'sweeter' the words, the 'more dangerous' they could be.[5]

On other occasions words are said to strike directly, as if they were weapons:

> ... these haughty words of hers
> Have batt'red me like roaring canon-shot.
> (*1 Henry VI*, III.iii.78–9)

> These words of yours draw life-blood from my heart.
>
> (Ibid., IV.vi.43)

> First let my words stab him, as he hath me.
>
> (*2 Henry VI*, IV.i.66)

> ... at each word's deliverance
> Stab poinards in our flesh till all were told,
> The words would add more anguish than the wounds
>
> (*3 Henry VI*, II.i.97–9)

> These words are razors to my wounded heart.
>
> (*Titus*, I.i.314)

> He speaks plain cannon-fire, and smoke and bounce;
> He gives the bastinado with his tongue;
> Our ears are cudgell'd; not a word of his
> But buffets better than a fist of France.
>
> (*John*, II.i. 462–5)

This last speech mocks the bravado of a warrior who 'bethumps' with words, as the speaker exchanges blow for blow with confident expertise.

In the early comedies, the energy of words carries the action forward and animates the confrontations. Just before the conclusion of *The Taming of the Shrew*, Katherine uses mixed metaphors so that the combat of words is also a game in which words are bandied back and forth:

> My mind hath been as big as one of yours,
> My heart as great, my reason haply more,
> To bandy word for word and frown for frown;
> But now I see or lances are but straws,
> Our strength as weak, our weakness past compare ...
>
> (V.ii.170–4)

Audiences may still differ about who wins and who loses in this comedy, but Shakespeare has made it very clear that words are combative and deceitful to the very last moment; his mind and art thrived on this very circumstance.

Shakespeare also knew the value of a simple vocabulary – 'Honest plain words best pierce the ear of grief'[6] – and took as much delight in a rock-hard 'yes' or 'no' as in the creation of a long line of hyperboles or brilliant conceits. He could make audiences laugh at three pedants employing 'gracious words', 'sweet and voluble ... discourse', 'high-born' and 'fire-new words', and all that was 'most singular and choice, ... well-culled, chose, sweet, and apt', but when they vie with each other most ridiculously in *Love's Labour's Lost*, using scraps they have stolen from a 'great feast of languages',[7] on stage with them he brings Dull the Constable, who knows none of all this. 'Via, goodman Dull' exclaims Holofernes, the zealous schoolmaster, 'Thou hast spoken no word all this while', at which Dull's simple reply – 'Nor understood none neither, sir'[8] – is nicely calculated by the author to redouble laughter at the extravagant vocabulary of the learned competitors.

Shakespeare's simplest writing can bear great weight; and it can be precise, speedy, subtle or resonant at will. A single syllable may be crucial or an easy and familiar phrase may be transformed into a statement of distinct individuality. In some of the comedies, a single word is begged or whispered as if life depended on it. In *Much Ado About Nothing*, Antonio denies his identity twice 'at a word', very deliberately; and then Benedick by far the wittier man, is forced to do the same thing, three times over without apology.[9] When Benedick is in pursuit of Beatrice, he becomes miserly with words in his own fashion: 'Old signior,' he explains to Leonato: 'walk aside with me; I have studied eight or nine wise words to speak to you, which these hobby-horses must not hear' (III.ii.63–5). Benedick and Beatrice are often extravagant in their use of words, but the moment when they come to trust each other is couched in short words, carefully placed:

BENEDICK Think you in your soul the Count Claudio hath wrong'd Hero?
BEATRICE Yea, as sure as I have a thought or a soul.
BENEDICK Enough, I am engag'd. ...

(IV.i.325–7)

In *The Merry Wives of Windsor*, the comic chase is more varied and less fraught, but it is often handled very cogently: 'at a word', 'a word with you', 'at a word', 'speak a good word', 'a word or two', 'a word with your ear'. Belief in the simple efficacy of a single word provides a running gag, and the comedy springs ahead whenever this trigger is touched.[10]

In *Measure for Measure*, written a few years later, characters struggle to use words in plain and honest sense. When Isabella begs Angelo to save her brother's life, a series of simple words takes the brunt of the argument:

ISABELLA   Must he needs *die*?
ANGELO   Maiden, no remedy.
ISABELLA   Yes; I do think that you might pardon him.
  And neither heaven nor man grieve at the mercy.
ANGELO   I will *not do't*.
ISABELLA   But *can* you, if you *would*?
ANGELO   Look, what I *will not*, that I *cannot* do.
ISABELLA   But *might* you do't, and do the world *no wrong*,
  If so your heart were touch'd with that remorse
  As mine is to him?
ANGELO   He's sentenc'd; 'tis *too late*.
LUCIO   You are *too cold*.

(II.ii.48–56)

Isabella's response is to question the power of the single word 'late'; and then her speech takes longer flight until she offers for the second time the single, but far more difficult, word 'mercy'. This is crucial, and a half-line suggests that she is silent for a moment and everyone else with her:

ISABELLA   Too late? Why, no; I, that do speak a word,
  May call it back again. Well, believe this:
  No ceremony that to great ones longs,
  Not the king's crown nor the deputed sword,
  The marshal's truncheon nor the judge's robe,
  Become them with one half so good a grace
  As mercy does.

Words that sound even more simple are now used, repeatedly, to drive the argument forward:

  If *he* had been as *you*, and *you* as *he*,
  You would have slipp'd like *him*; but *he*, like *you*,
  Would not have been so stern.

In contrast with simple pronouns and the verb 'to be,' 'slipp'd' and 'stern' gain delicate emphasis, so that they invite rather than press for acceptance. Angelo's only reply is worded with utmost simplicity: 'Pray you be gone.' Under insistent pressure a familiar phrase here takes all the strain. It can be spoken and acted in many ways, but in all of them simple words suggest great feeling and particular intention. 'Honest plain words' can hardly describe speech in such a context, but it may serve as reminder that Shakespeare's choice of words was not invariably fine, rare, brave, splendid, or consciously poetic. He also used ordinary words brilliantly.

The ability of simple-seeming words to represent complex matters was often a source of interest for Shakespeare, and in the history plays and tragedies such words are frequently teased, stretched, and tested almost to destruction. In *King John* the word 'death' is approached with hesitation and it is followed by a series of weighted words to ensure that it is fully comprehended:

KING   Good Hubert, Hubert, Hubert, throw thine eye
   On yon young boy. I'll tell thee what, my friend,
   He is a very serpent in my way;
   And wheresoe'er this foot of mine doth tread,
   He lies before me. Dost thou understand me?
   Thou art his keeper.
HUBERT   And I'll keep him so
   That he shall not offend your Majesty.
KING   Death.
HUBERT   My lord?
KING   A grave.
HUBERT   He shall not live.
KING   Enough!
                                             (III.iii.59–69)

Speech is here under great and various pressures. Differences in arrangement of the verse-lines and choice of punctuation which are to be found in modern editions indicate something of its difficulty. Is there a question mark after Hubert's 'My lord'? Does 'Enough' call for an exclamation mark? Do the five short phrases from 'Death' to 'Enough' represent one verse-line or two? The last question is vital, because a long pause before or after 'Death' alters the force of several words and the willingness with which each character accepts the crime of murdering Prince Arthur. Once Hubert is committed to his purpose, the King veers away to a series of short statements:

> I could be merry now. Hubert, I love thee.
> Well, I'll not say what I intend for thee.
> Remember. [*He turns to his mother.*] Madam, fare you well;
> I'll send those powers o'er to your Majesty.

'Merry' and 'love' may now sound like overstatements; the negative 'I'll not say' may seem fearful, and the single word 'Remember' can be reassuring or threatening. Immediately afterwards, the King turns away from this 'good' man whom he has just promised to 'love'; and Hubert says nothing more, not even when Arthur is committed to his charge. From a crucial and careful use of simple words, Shakespeare has moved on to use the same means to give an impression of uncertainty and instability; plain, everyday words cover, rather than reveal, the true force of feeling.

In comic pursuit, keen dispute, argument, or political machination, single words are drawn into prominence by the force of dramatic action, their effectiveness built up by repetition or secured by contrasting developments. But in other scenes a single and everyday word can signal absolute change, as if it were a token of intention and, at the same time, an absolutely satisfactory vessel for deep and pent-up feelings. So, for example, in *Henry the Fourth, Part Two*, the dying king believes that Hal is treacherous and thinks only of inheriting his crown and power: he reproves his son for folly, ambition, a stony heart, and lawlessness, but then listens to the young man's defence. Hal's words grow in confidence and feeling, and he finishes with a solemn prayer. His father is silent throughout all this protestation, but then after a further and shared silence come the words 'O my son': they alone, in all their simplicity, effect reconciliation and carry massive implications of forgiveness, acceptance, and dawning happiness. Soon the king can continue:

> Come hither, Harry; sit thou by my bed,
> And hear, I think, the very latest counsel
> That ever I shall breathe.
>
> (IV.v.178–84)

What follows is the father's reappraisal of his whole life, admitting the 'indirect crook'd ways' (l. 185) by which he usurped the crown of England. His speech grows weaker – 'my lungs are wasted so That strength of speech is utterly denied me' (ll. 216–17) – but he struggles to make an end, using two full lines in which all the words are 'plain' and 'honest', and so simple that only one, the most crucial and uncertain, is more than a monosyllable:

> How came I by the crown, O God, forgive;
> And grant it may with thee in true peace live!
> (ll. 219–20)

Another shared silence follows, and then Hal chooses a royal address, 'My gracious liege', before he can reassure his father. He begins by using plain, if not entirely honest, words, but then, as the king had done, he concludes with more political niceties and larger concepts:

> My gracious liege,
> You won it, wore it, kept it, gave it me;
> Then *plain* and *right* must my possession be;
> Which I with more than with a common pain
> 'Gainst all the world will rightfully maintain.
> (ll. 221–5)

*   *   *

Plain and honest words, silence, wordless exclamations are at one end of the spectrum of Shakespeare's vocabulary, while at the other are strange, new, transformed words that in his own day were hard to understand, and also sequences of words that sounded as if written on purpose to 'grace harmony' and amaze their hearers. Shakespeare's invention quickened as he wrote and sometimes the energy of his thought seems to be present in the text beyond the limits of dramatic credibility or the necessities of action. Especially in early plays, some of the speeches grow to a climax in which pleasure of invention threatens to overwhelm strict sense and lead all but the most artful speakers to finish breathlessly. This writing has vitality and resource, brilliance and subtlety, and shows a relaxed and seemingly inexhaustible power. The delight with which it was composed and the delight with which it needs to be spoken are both transmitted to the audience. Such versatility raises the play towards greater excitement, as though its text had become music and its performance dance, moving into some other form of communication than an imitation of the speech of men and women. In such a game of skill, no side need ever win; all the competitors join in a celebration of language and of play.

Rhetoricians taught how to build speeches and manipulate argument, and lawyers, preachers, prose writers and poets all depended heavily on this underpinning and provided everyday examples of its use. Shakespeare was well acquainted with these skills, but was less interested in the manipulation of these structures than in the quickening energies of words. Scholars can identify anthypophora, apodioxis, paronomasia, parrhesia, gnome, and many other figures of rhetoric in Shakespeare's plays, but his quick invention tended to leap over all such slow decrees. In fact every reference to rhetoric and figures of speech in the plays is tinged with ridicule or suspicion. Words, and not rhetoricians' rules and structures, provided Shakespeare with pleasure and refreshment, and suggested his phrases and patterns of thought. They carried his mind forward and enabled him to give the impression that his characters were alive in the inward working of their own minds.

The plays are alight with verbal invention. Young men went to *Romeo and Juliet* to copy down phrases to use in their own adventures,[11] and fellow dramatists echoed his speeches in their own plays. Many of Shakespeare's phrases were immediately so memorable that they found their way quickly into everyday speech and became proverbs and familiar sayings in almost every walk of life. Yet his fertile invention left some hearers and readers unable to follow and at a loss to understand. In their address 'To the great variety of readers', prefixed to the first collected edition of Shakespeare's plays in 1623, Heminges and Condell, two actor-sharers of the King's Men, acknowledged that effort was needed to respond fully to these plays:

> . . . we hope, to your divers capacities, you will find enough both to draw and hold you: for his wit can no more lie hid than it could be lost. Read him, therefore; and again, and again: and if then you do not like him, surely you are in some manifest

danger not to understand him. And so we leave you to other of his friends whom, if you need, can be your guides. If you need them not, you can lead yourselves and others. And such readers we wish him.

On the wing – a phrase which Shakespeare is thought to have used for the first time – his invention drew upon a great wealth of meaning, reference, allusion, music, rhythmic energy. He seems to have soared effortlessly over a wide world of thought and feeling, commanding every prospect. One thought takes fire from another, to be displaced just as quickly.

Towards the end of *Henry and Fourth, Part One*, as battle draws near, the rebel Hotspur turns away from talk about the king to mock his rival, Prince Harry:

> Where is his son,
> The nimble-footed madcap Prince of Wales,
> And his comrades that daff'd the world aside
> And bid it pass?
>
> (IV.i.94–7)

From quick epithets deriding the folly and perhaps the cowardice of Harry, Hotspur places him on a wider stage and brings the casual and the global into ludicrous conjunction. Yet the phrase 'daff'd the world aside' has also a sense of heroic ease and it is this perhaps which has led many authors to appropriate it for their own use. The transitive verb 'daff' had earlier been used for putting off clothes, but here its more general connotation of saying farewell leads on to 'bid it pass'; and this, in turn, introduces a hint of death in an echo of 'let him pass'[12] and 'pass away'. (For Shakespeare 'daff', in the sense of taking off clothes, may have held the seed for Hamlet's later and yet more famous 'shuffled off this mortal coil'.) The mind of Shakespeare, inventing Hotspur's speech, has moved on, from mockery to heroic élan; and has also been touched – perhaps silenced – by thoughts of death.

In reply, Sir Richard Vernon starts directly and forcibly, but from the simple facts of military preparation he moves forward to similes and metaphors, a figurative elaboration which plunges and dips with athletic pleasure:

> All furnish'd, all in arms;
> All plum'd like estridges, that with the wind
> Bated like eagles having lately bath'd;
> Glittering in golden coats, like images;
> As full of spirit as the month of May
> And gorgeous as the sun at midsummer;
> Wanton as youthful goats, wild as young bulls.
>
> (ll. 97–103)

This speech is not a careful rhetorical description but grows out of resources implicit in its words. The sight of feathers decorating helmets leads on to image of ostriches and goshawks ('estridges' was used of both), and then on to 'eagles', beating their wings and breasting the air high over men's heads. For a moment the birds are still, and then the soldiers are remembered 'glittering' in sunshine, and so 'images' or effigies flash into imaginary view. Then these emblems of the spiritual life are displaced by a more general memory of the fresh season of May, until that impression yields to a full summer 'sun' and splendid unruliness. 'Goats' and 'bulls' tie thoughts down into more compact images and then a change of sentence-structure signals the end of this line of thought and sensation. Perhaps rampant sexuality offers such possibilities that an abrupt change is needed to avoid saying more. But the energy is not dissipated; all is superseded in one bound by a closer look at the leader of these comrades. Again the start is matter-of-fact:

> I saw young Harry with his beaver on,
> His cushes on his thighs, gallantly arm'd,
> Rise from the ground like feathered Mercury,
> And vaulted with such ease into his seat
> As if an angel dropp'd down from the clouds
> To turn and wind a fiery Pegasus,
> And witch the world with noble horsemanship.
>
> (ll. 104–10)

Prodigious physical strength would be needed to vault into a saddle while wearing full armour – ordinary men would use a mounting block or at least a helping arm – but as he wrote of this Shakespeare gave Harry a further god-like comparison, with Mercury – mythical and, once more, high in the air above men's heads, as if the vaulting were a levitation. Then 'angel' makes the image holy once more, but 'dropp'd down' is a mundane turn of phrase which in this context seems almost comic, certainly unpompous. Then as Harry is described putting his mount through the formal paces of the 'manage', 'witching' restores the earlier sense of mystery, but in less pious terms.

Commentary labours clumsily after such writing, but only by attempting to follow the movements in Shakespeare's mind, as one image leads to another, can we begin to measure its energies – its speed, reach, variety of weight and focus, and sensitivity. Such writing seems, indeed, to 'rise above the ground' and command with bewitching ease. Words were infinite riches in the mind of Shakespeare: in possession of this treasure he lived like a lord, and was noble, generous, and free. He was, by turns, learnedly ingenious and openly sensitive to ordinary experience:

> his delights
> Were dolphin-like: they show'd his back above
> The element they lived in. In his livery
> Walk'd crowns and crownets; realms and islands were
> As plates dropp'd from his pocket.
> (*Antony and Cleopatra*, V.ii.88–92)

The odds are that Shakespeare had never seen a 'dolphin', but he had read about them and imagined them with Arion or a mermaid riding on their backs; and he also knew 'Dolphin' as a name for a french knight, a dog, and a chamber in a tavern. Liveries he had seen in plenty and, by the time he wrote this, he had walked in the coronation procession of James I dressed in a suit of the new king's livery. As 'crowns' could stand in for their wearers in his mind, so territorial possessions became crown-coins, or 'plates' spilt from a 'pocket'; and so focus and scale change once again, and everyday occurrences mingle with fabulous fantasies.

Two contrasted passages, written for every different characters and situations, exemplify the energy and feeling with which Shakespeare could write about the use of words. When Falstaff praises sherris-sack, he claims that the operation of this drink is the promotion of verbal wit:

It ascends me into the brain; dries me there all the foolish and
dull and crudy vapours which environ it; makes it apprehensive, quick, forgetive, full of nimble, fiery, and delectable shapes;
which delivered o'er to the voice, the tongue, which is the birth,
becomes excellent wit.   (*2 Henry IV*, IV.iii.94–8)

Falstaff has just captured a 'famous rebel', and so his words may
well reflect the writer's own enthusiasm in confident and buoyant mood. On the other hand, when Mowbray is banished from
England by King Richard, whom he has served faithfully at the
risk of his own honour, his sense of deprivation may reflect Shakespeare's own feelings when power over words deserted him and
he was unable to write:

> The language I have learnt these forty years,
> My native English, now I must forgo;
> And now my tongue's use is to me no more
> Than an unstringed viol or a harp;
> Or like a cunning instrument cas'd up
> Or, being open, put into his hands
> That knows no touch to tune the harmony.
> (*Richard II*, I.iii.159–65)

Words awakened Shakespeare's imagination so that all manner of experiences were both remembered and set free in new
associations and new forms. Every sensation was involved: sight,
sound, touch, taste, and occasionally smell. A speaker's physical
well-being, sexuality, memory, and immediate apprehension and
activity, could all be activated by words, reflected in them, and
to some extent changed by them. Speech was related to physical
sensation, as readily as to intention, emotion, or intellectual thought,
and so was able to suggest a heightened mode of existence, capable
of greater precision and wider extension than actual life; it could
turn speech into music, thought into a waking, lively, and almost
palpable dream. Such is the message contained in Theseus's account of imagination – a speech carefully emended at least once
by Shakespeare – towards the end of *A Midsummer Night's Dream*,
before the play of Pyramus and Thisbe was performed in his
presence.

Lovers and madmen have such seething brains,
Such shaping fantasies, that apprehend
More than cool reason ever comprehends.
The lunatic, the lover, and the poet,
Are of imagination all compact.
One sees more devils than vast hell can hold;
That is the madman. The lover, all as frantic,
Sees Helen's beauty in a brow of Egypt.
The poet's eye, in a fine frenzy rolling,
Doth glance from heaven to earth, from earth to heaven;
And as imagination bodies forth
The forms of things unknown, the poet's pen
Turns them to shapes, and gives to airy nothing
A local habitation and a name.
Such tricks hath strong imagination
That, if it would but apprehend some joy,
It comprehends some bringer of that joy;
Or in the night, imagining some fear,
How easy is a bush suppos'd a bear?

(V.i.4–22)

Theseus is not Shakespeare, but such a view of a poet's imagination is in accordance with the way he wrote, especially in the earlier plays, and it provides a useful way of trying to account for the effectiveness of the texts. An imaginative response is called for, rather than a pursuit of any meaning, theme, or argument which can be rigorously defined. Bushes and bears should both be expected, and also whatever is unique in our individual enjoyment of the plays. A reader or critic who has not been amazed by what words awaken in the mind cannot begin to respond to what Shakespeare has written.

*   *   *

Words cannot be treated as isolated linguistic phenomena and no writer can be judged by vocabulary alone. Phonology, syntax and semantics are involved in any usage; and relationships between words, syntagmatic and paradigmatic, are as significant as the definition of separate linguistic forms. Words, we know, are only one element in speech and never contain its whole meaning.

Nevertheless, if we wish to understand how Shakespeare thought about his own writing, 'word' is the word to use wherever possible, and we should try to develop our understanding from this beginning. His characters talk about communication between people by considering their words; they also speak of 'talk', 'speech', 'chat', 'prattle', 'style', 'poetry', 'sign', 'figure', 'epithet', but none of these alternatives occurs so frequently as 'word' and 'words'. The Bible tells how Adam learned to speak by giving names to the natural phenomena of the newly created world, and Shakespeare's contemporaries revered the arts of writing and speech as proper developments of this primal process. Admittedly Biblical authority was being questioned closely and each definition of truth or of God was being pitted against others, so that simple confidence in the efficacy of words could hardly be expected among people of any education. But this only makes it more remarkable that the older and habitual respect was slow to change and continued to influence thought. To write or speak well, it was said, one should seek out the proper and apt word for each occasion. In a reprint of 1585, Sir Thomas Wilson's *Art of Rhetoric* could still imply that words are secure and reliable:

> Such are thought apt words, that properly agree unto that thing which they signify, and plainly express the nature of the same. Therefore they that have regard of their estimation do warily speak and, with choice, utter words most apt for their purpose. (pp. 165–6)

Shakespeare's attitude to words was never that simple and became progressively more complex and uneasy. Perhaps laughter prevented any great confidence, because puns, jokes, and absurdity in the plays modify the effect of words surprisingly. In *The Merchant of Venice*, written around 1596, Shakespeare has Lorenzo comment twice on the clown's way with words:

> How every fool can play upon the word! I think the best grace of wit will shortly turn into silence, and discourse grow commendable in none only but parrots. (III.v.38–40)

> > O dear discretion, how his words are suited!
> > The fool hath planted in his memory

An army of good words; and I do know
A many fools that stand in better place,
Garnish'd like him, that for a tricksy word
Defy the matter.   (ll. 56–61)

In the very next scene, after the fool's mocking words have been appraised so carefully, Portia will stand in front of the Duke of Venice to wrest a meaning from the words of Shylock's bond which neither her husband Bassanio, nor anybody else, had thought of when they tried to save Antonio's life. Shakespeare may also betray his own concern about 'tricksy' words when Lorenzo turns from talking about the fool to ask his bride, Jessica, for a verbal judgement:

How cheer'st thou, Jessica?
And now, good sweet, say thy opinion,
How dost thou like the Lord Bassanio's wife?
                                    (ll. 61–3)

Jessica has been silent for some time, and it is notable that she still has nothing to say even when Lorenzo asks 'how cheer'st thou?' When he again presses his second question, her first instinct is to refuse a second time because all she can say at first is that her thoughts on the subject are 'past all expressing' (l. 64).

The Merchant of Venice of 1596 shows that Shakespeare's attitude to words had changed. By now he was concerned with the inexpressible and with the many ways in which words 'defy the matter'. The very first lines of this comedy speak of feelings which are not to be trusted to words:

ANTONIO In sooth, I know not why I am so sad.
It wearies me; you say it wearies you . . .

Before long his companions are playing with words and laughing at their own verbal wit or at Antonio's lack of it. When he deflects Solanio's 'Why then you are in love' with a curt 'Fie, fie!', the following jokes appear to turn more openly against his unsmiling and mostly silent reception of their good counsel and mockery. Throughout this comedy there are moments when words are manifestly unable to present all that is afoot. Bassanio is uneasy at the bond Shylock proposes: 'I like not fair terms and a villain's mind' (I.iii.174). When Bassanio has won Portia as his wife by a correct reading of her father's riddles, he uses words only to confess the inexpressible, the coursing of blood in his veins and the 'wild of nothing' which joy brings to his inner self:

> Madam, you have bereft me of all words;
> Only my blood speaks to you in my veins;
> And there is such confusion in my powers
> As, after some oration fairly spoke
> By a beloved prince, there doth appear
> Among the buzzing pleased multitude,
> Where every something, being blent together,
> Turns to a wild of nothing, save of joy
> Express'd and not expressed!
>
> (III.ii.176–84)

Shylock's exit as he leaves the court after his defeat in the trial is always a notable moment in a performance of the play, yet here no words at all were used by Shakespeare to set the seal on one of the most eloquent roles he had ever created by this stage of his career. In the last Act Jessica is also mysterious in silence: she speaks very few words and everyone speaks of her as if they expect to hear nothing from her. When Antonio receives his wealth back again, laughter becomes general as in amazement and pleasure he announces, simply, 'I am dumb' (l. 279).

Later comedies exploit with growing skill the inexpressible and the possibility of false interpretations. In *As You Like It* Rosalind's disguise as Ganymede invites a great train of double meanings which draw her ever more deeply into thoughts she would not otherwise express. In *Much Ado About Nothing* the entire plot depends on words that are misunderstood. Claudio and Don Pedro are convinced by words falsely spoken in the dark; and 'blushing apparitions' on Hero's face are needed to establish her 'maiden truth'.[13] Benedick and Beatrice are tricked by other people's words into declaring mutual love. In the exchanges between these two after Claudio has denounced Hero on her wedding day, some words are doubted and the meaning of others insisted upon – and all so strenuously that an audience is torn between laughter and concern. The tone of this scene is notoriously difficult, and perhaps the only certainty in performance is that the two speakers are very much in earnest, using words as best they can and changing from one to another with both passion and insecurity.

In *Twelfth Night*, written around 1600, when Shakespeare has brought his heroine, Viola, to be alone with Feste the fool, their talk is almost all about words:

> FESTE   To see this age! A sentence is but a chev'ril glove to a good wit. How quickly the wrong side may be turn'd outward!
> VIOLA   Nay, that's certain; they that dally nicely with words may quickly make them wanton.
> FESTE   I would, therefore, my sister had had no name, sir.
> VIOLA   Why, man?
> FESTE   Why, sir, her name's a word; and to dally with that word might make my sister wanton. But indeed words are very rascals since bonds[14] disgrac'd them.
> VIOLA   Thy reason, man?
> FESTE   Troth, sir, I can yield you none without words, and words are grown so false I am loath to prove reason with them.
>
> (III.i.10–22)

Here Shakespeare has created characters who know that words have no virtue which is able to resist misusage: all that is said may signify nothing, or nearly so. The exchange continues enigmatically:

> VIOLA   I warrant thou art a merry fellow and car'st for nothing.
> FESTE   Not so, sir; I do care for something; but in my conscience, sir, I do not care for you. If that be to care for nothing, sir, I would it would make you invisible.

From this moment impetus recovers as Viola calls Feste a fool, but here, as elsewhere in this comedy, behind the talk an audience may perceive that words mean only what the speaker or hearer wills. Behind the foolery can be glimpsed an exploration of sexual fantasy and personal confidence. Context and use define meaning, not the wanton words themselves.

In *The Tragedy of Hamlet*, written about a year after *Twelfth Night*, and also in subsequent plays, Shakespeare searched out this new awareness – 'There is nothing', says Hamlet, 'either good or bad but thinking makes it so' – and 'indirections' often seem the appropriate way to 'find directions out'.[15] Hamlet 'unpacks [his] heart with words' and is so ready to 'prate of mountains' –

> an thou'lt mouth,
I'll rant as well as thou –

that the Queen, his mother, calls his behaviour 'mere madness', a 'fit' that will a while 'work on him'.[16] Words, in this play, are not only deceptive, whirling, and mad; they also return to wound the speaker:

> Hamlet is of the faction that is wrong'd;
> His madness is poor Hamlet's enemy.
> (V.ii.230–1)

By the end of the action Claudius seeks an 'hour of quiet' and Hamlet seems to welcome the 'silence' of death; he had already foreseen death as a 'quietus',[17] that is, a quittance for debt and also, in a 'tricksy' sense, a 'quiet'.

In the great tragedies words are tested to breaking point as they possess and deceive their users. Earlier Falstaff had played with the notion that 'Honour' was a 'word' only, 'air' and nothing substantial, and so he lived with his cowardice and kept a 'confident brow' and a 'throng of words' to protect his own interests.[18] Still earlier, around 1595, Shakespeare had given Richard II a soliloquy in which he set himself to 'hammer . . . out' his thoughts and

> set the word itself
Against the word.
> (V.v.1–41)

But Hamlet, Othello, Macbeth and Lear all fight strenuously to find words which can accompany and sustain them to the very end. Perhaps for these plays the more illuminating question for a critic is not about what their leading characters say or do, but about the ways in which they use words in the last resort.

Hamlet's very first speeches question the meaning and force of words but, when the First Player seems carried away by speaking of the 'mobbled queen', he is tempted to 'unpack' his heart with words.[19] Just before the end of the play, when he counters the elaborate speech of Osric by assuming its own manner, he understands very well the dangerous nature of the invitation this courtier brings; he knows too that Osric's double-talk is a sign of the times:

Thus has he, and many more of the same bevy, that I know the drossy age dotes on, only got the tune of the time and outward habit of encounter – a kind of yesty collection, which carries them through and through the most fann'd and winnowed opinions; and do but blow them to their trial, the bubbles are out. (V.ii.183–8)

Does this mean that Shakespeare with Hamlet no longer trusts words? A simple negative or afirmative to that question would be ridiculous, but this question does arise from his presentation of Hamlet, and it persists in the plays that followed. Hamlet speaks of a kind of theatre in which 'the players cannot keep counsel; they'll tell all',[20] but that is not the mode which Shakespeare was starting to invent.

Shakespeare used words for both statement and evasion, to expose and to conceal the nature of his characters. The plays themselves alert us to these contrasted methods. So, in *Hamlet*, Claudius acknowledges that his potent words have flown up towards heaven while his 'thoughts remain below',[21] and Angelo in *Measure for Measure* acknowledges:

When I would pray and think, I think and pray
To several subjects. Heaven hath my empty words,
Whilst my invention, hearing not my tongue,
Anchors on Isabel. Heaven in my mouth,
As if I did but only chew his name,
And in my heart the strong and swelling evil
Of my conception.

(II.iv.1–7)

At times Shakespeare wrote in scorn of words and their ability to express what he knew of human experience. Nowhere is this more obvious than in the comparatively early narrative poem *The Rape of Lucrece* (1583–4). The wronged heroine is speaking:

Out, idle words, servants to shallow fools!
Unprofitable sounds, weak arbitrators!
Busy yourselves in skill-contending schools,
Debate where leisure serves with dull debaters;
To trembling clients be you mediators.

> For me, I force not argument a straw,
> Since that my case is past the help of law.
>
> In vain I rail at Opportunity,
> At Time, at Tarquin, and uncheerful Night;
> In vain I cavil with mine infamy,
> In vain I spurn at my confirm'd despite:
> *This helpless smoke of words doth me no right.*
>   The remedy indeed to do me good
>   Is to let forth my foul defiled blood.
>
> (ll. 1016–29)

Shakespeare's imagination was quickened by using words but from early in his career he knew that words could become a 'helpless smoke' which effected nothing that would satisfy a speaker. Slowly, but with increasing boldness, he developed this awareness and so found the means to create plays which are alive with deeply felt experience beyond the reach of words and with suggestions of multiple levels of consciousness. To appreciate Shakespeare's art, we must pay strict attention to the words he used, but we must also look through them to a more complete impression of thoughts and feelings that lie beneath them and indeed motivate them.

This is not an easy idea for a reader or a literary critic to digest, especially since both may have been drawn to Shakespeare's plays in the first place by the brilliance of the words alone. But here words are never alone. They are part of a fuller experience. As they are spoken, any force, colour, association, reference, and, of course, meaning they may have had on a previous occasion will all change as they become part of another complex and shifting phenomenon. Words should not be taken out of their context in a play by Shakespeare. Left by themselves, in simple quotation, they can say nothing very useful about the lively image of life which that play presents and they can provide no adequate statement of meaning. Both reader and critic should also direct their attention somewhere else, through the words and behind the words.

3
Speech and Action

Words alone do not bring a play to life; the persons who speak them have to come alive too. Until we observe how Shakespeare achieved this, we have not responded as fully as we might to what he has written. Behind the words on a page lies an imagined reality in which each character is activated distinctively, so that they all appear to be in independent charge of what they say and do.

On stage, a play releases its true nature. Henry Irving used to say that this happened when an actor was 'moved by the impulse of being';[1] having studied a part as carefully as possible, with a leap of imagination he made the character his own. Thoughts hidden under words, sensuous activity of all kinds, reactions to time and place, interactions with other characters and with the events of each moment as they occur, every element of lived experience: all this is caught up in the heightened and cunning form of life which is a play in performance. Every actor brings individual qualities and experience to this task, so that a play does not have one realisation on stage but many, each achieved by using the same script but following different routes and using different talents and techniques.

Shakespeare was an actor as well as author, so that he knew the processes of collaboration which would bring his plays before their audiences. As he wrote, he thought as an actor, in part at least, so that embodied in his scripts are millions of clues which performers can search out and use in their work, and they are as useful today as when the plays were first written. It is an almost incredible fact that, even now, actors speak as if Shakespeare were himself present at rehearsals, ready to guide, support and energise. Laurence Olivier put it like this:

> The great parts – you've no idea how they devour you. You are playing Othello, God! You give it all you've got. The author

says to you: 'You've given it all you've got? Good. Now, more . . . Good! You've done that? Fine. Now more! More, damn you, more! *more*! MORE! M–O–R–E!!' And your heart and your guts and your brain are pulp, and the part feeds on them. Acting great parts devours you. Great parts are cannibals. It is a danger-ous game.[2]

No two actors will present the same Othello on stage, but the common experience of all who take on Shakespeare's roles, both great and small, is that, if they pay close attention to the text, the author not only seems to direct and support them; he also spurs them on to discover more and more about their characters in performance.

If we wish to understand a play by Shakespeare, we have to consider how words suggest 'impulse[s] of being' with which the actors can take over the play and work on it with heightened and inspired energy. Many practical directions are to be found in the smallest linguistic details of the text. John Gielgud explained how:

> I try to study the sound, shape and length of words themselves, so as to reproduce them exactly as they are written on the page. In a verse speech (and often in a long prose one too) I am constantly aware of the whole span of the arc – the beginning, middle and end of the passage. I try to phrase correctly for breathing, punctuation and emphasis, and then, conforming to this main line, I experiment within it for modulation, tone, and pace, trying not to drag out the vowels, elongate syllables, or pounce on opening phrases, and being very careful not to drop the ends of words and sentences and to pronounce the final consonants – D, T, P, and so forth.[3]

'Good verse-speaking', wrote John Gielgud, 'is rather like swim-ming. If you surrender to the water it keeps you up, but if you fight you drown.'[4]

Attention to pronunciation and speech can shape a performance without providing an intellectual concept or insisting upon any particular meaning for word or gesture. The actor gains a secu-rity of mind in which to trust the less manageable forces of pas-sion and fantasy. 'The joke is', said Sir John, 'that people think of me as an intellectual actor. Yet I have always trusted almost entirely to observation, emotion and instinct. In the theatre, I cannot help being very emotional.'[5]

Other actors do not rely so much on 'good verse-speaking', but have their own ways of watching and waiting for inspiration, working on the text. Ralph Richardson reflected that:

> It's fascinating what part of your body *feels* right when you're preparing a role.... I sometimes find it starts in my ... *feet*. You can feel secure in your feet. The role comes gradually with various parts of the body. It doesn't fill the anatomy at once. Sometimes the voice is behind. Other times, I feel very secure in my ... *eyes*.[6]

Normally this would be long after he knew the text of his part by heart and had worked for many hours on his own as well as in company rehearsals.

Peggy Ashcroft used to say that two distinct ways of working were needed to complement each other:

> It's like the chicken and the egg. You can appreciate a line, but it's no good thinking you know how to say it until you've found the character. Only when we have the character are we able to say the line as it should be said. Not by everybody, or anybody, but by us, because we've made that particular character. So it has to fit with that, and then it comes out naturally.[7]

'Finding the character' is crucial, and each actor has to search for it independently, bringing every talent and experience to bear upon the task and so ensuring that each impersonation is unique – unique in itself and in its relationship to Shakespeare's text.

While working in public sessions with members of his theatre company, Peter Brook explained why he advised starting work on a text by paying attention to words:

> There is a dynamic movement in words and, as you discover it, you grasp the real movement of a character. A large part of inspiration is hidden in letters and syllables, when it isn't in the placing of words, in their way of answering through a monologue.[8]

When an actor finds what is useable for himself or herself, the result is a new interpretation. But this does not imply that Shakespeare was weak or uncertain in purpose as he wrote. Such a variety is possible because his mind focused on the inner beings of his characters, rather than on their outwardly visible physique or their past history. The inner life of the characters is of primary importance to an actor, even before their significance in the argument of a play or in the working out of its narrative. This imagined existence is expressed by the words Shakespeare set down and the actions those words imply. So his characters are implicit in the texts waiting to be realised. Feet, voice, eyes, head, hands, body – every faculty, power and expressive means – can be activated by the 'impulse of being' supplied by each interpreter working with the words that have been set down.

It is amazing how precise an actor can become in defining what he or she has found in the text. The imagined being comes into existence proportioned, clothed, and delineated with great exactness; often a past history is furnished and a future predicated. This is what Donald Sinden had to say about his Malvolio:

> I see him as a military man; unpopular at school, he joins the army and, while he displays no quality of leadership, he is so damned efficient that he now finds himself, at forty-five, a Colonel in the Pay corps, embittered, with no prospect of further promotion. He has bored every woman he has met and he stays unmarried. A certain widowed Count I suppose needed a major-domo to manage his Mediterranean estate, and who better than this totally efficient and honest teetotaller?[9]

As inevitable conclusions which anyone might draw from the text, these inventions can be dismissed very quickly. But it does not follow that they are wrong for this particular actor or irrelevant to our understanding of the plays. Shakespeare's text can suggest such infrastructures with quite unusual ease. It engenders multitudes of them, each one invented by an actor as an aid in giving physical and psychological reality to the imagined being which seems to lie within the text.

When Paul Scofield reviewed Maynard Mack's *King Lear in Our Time* (1965), some three years after he had acted the leading role, he took issue with the scholar's view that Shakespeare paid little attention to 'the psychological processes that ordinarily precede or determine human action'. Scofield insisted that, as an actor, he had no option but to honour the specific mortal nature of the man he represents. An archetype cannot be acted, just as a performance cannot be written.

Professor Mack's arguments that Shakespeare's characters are 'implausible' or 'absurd' he countered very simply: an actor must either trust Shakespeare or lose touch with the centre of his character's life and the play's deepest interests:

> If we are to be impatient of paradoxes in the behaviour of Shakespeare's characters, or frustrated by their often enigmatic personalities, then the heart of his plays is lost to us. In the major roles of all the great plays there is a seeming contradiction of purpose or ambiguity of character; it is only by the acceptance of paradox as being intrinsic to human behaviour that Lear or Hamlet, Othello or Macbeth can be more than objects of intellectual analysis.[10]

Phrases like 'psychological processes' were unknown to Shakespeare's generation, but that does not mean that he was unable to understand a 'specific mortal nature' or the conflicts and contradictions of inner consciousness. The texts refer to unexpected and incommunicable thoughts often enough – 'There's no art to find the mind's construction in the face' – and to irrational behaviour which cannot be held in check – 'the imperfections of long-engraffed condition'.[11] They require an actor to show the involuntary onset of madness, everyday absent-mindedness, or spontaneous eruptions of vituperation or wit. Moreover, Richard Burbage, the first creator of many of Shakespeare's greatest roles, was said to become so immersed in a character that he was

> a delightful Proteus, so wholly transforming himself into his part, and putting off himself with his clothes, as he never (not so much as in the tyring-house) assum'd himself again until the play was done.[12]

Experience has led actors to believe that individual human beings lie within the words of Shakespeare's text ready for them to discover and assume in their performances, and this confidence should have huge repercussions on any attempt to understand the nature of what Shakespeare wrote in his plays. Alerted and energised by the power and danger of words, Shakespeare created a world peopled by imaginary beings who are like people in ordinary life but operate in a more intense mode; they are also capable of being realised in many different forms. No analysis of language or style, no concept of character or theory about what the plays mean, no definition of argument, narrative, or critique of society, no intellectual perception, can reveal a play's full life to us. Shakespeare was a practical and imaginative writer whose works have to be experienced as images of a life in which individual persons have their distinctive beings: he wrote for performance.

*   *   *

The vitality of Shakespeare's characters in performance testifies to the freedom of his conception and the openness of his text. Lear, Benedick, Rosalind, Malvolio, Dull the Constable, Desdemona, Iago and Othello, together with the nameless Apothecary, Priests and Messengers, have all appeared in new guises each time the plays have been staged, and in almost all these variations actors have carried conviction. Such liberty in interpretation implies no disrespect for the unchanging words on the page: the characters have been conceived in such a way that they invite many and varied manifestations.

Shakespeare was not restricted by the way in which any particular performer – including himself – might have acted any part. Occasionally personal looks and physical characteristics are mentioned in the texts. Rosaline in *Love's Labour's Lost* should have dark eyes and hair, Portia in *The Merchant of Venice* golden hair. Rosalind and Helena are tall, Hermia and Hero short, and a few minor roles must be played by a notably thin actor. The appearance of the Apothecary in *Romeo and Juliet*, Adam in *As You Like It*, and Caliban in *The Tempest*, of Richard the Third, King Lear, Othello and other 'Moors', are all described with some exactness, but many actors could provide these mere externals by costume, make-up, wig, and performance. Twins should have some easily recognised feature in common, and the same clothing. Some parts call for very young actors, or those who are physically strong or heavy-weight. But after such exceptions have been acknowledged, it remains generally true that the individuality of Shakespeare's characters depends almost wholly on the workings of body and mind, not on physique or individual feature. This does not mean that all actors will be equally suited to all roles, but that age-range, talent, temperament, and imagination will be the main criteria for casting any part.

Actors queue up for the opportunity to perform in these plays because it is almost wholly pleasurable to learn what to do with a speech by Shakespeare, and to discover how to make each 'moment' work in terms of a new production and one's own abilities. As an actor begins to 'possess' a character, individual physical skill, voice, sensibility, memories, dreams and a lively response to present-day realities, are all drawn into the performance; and the text seems to grow in power and effectiveness. The actor discovers 'the reason' why Shakespeare wrote in these rhythms, why he chose this word or that, why a line is funny, or why some information is withheld or misconstrued – or, rather, the actor will *believe* that he or she begins to have this very specialised knowledge. As rehearsals progress and performances follow, actors may become more daring and seem on the brink of still further discoveries. Yet a time will come, almost invariably, when they grow dissatisfied: there are possibilities that have not been explored, a sense that all has not been achieved. The text remains inexhaustible and, to some degree, mysterious. How Shakespeare was able to write in this way is one of the deepest secrets of his art. Somehow he must have envisioned each role from within, sensing every reaction and impulse; then – or possibly at the same time – he was able to express this imaginary life by the use of written words alone. Sensation and thought are held within Shakespeare's web of words and that subtle fabric becomes a garment which many generations of actors have worn to their own advantages.

But the text as a garment is not an adequate image. Shakespeare's words become part of the inner life of the actor; they are not simply an external covering. We can think of the text as a framework for the mind, a mental skeleton which imposes certain thought-processes and controls physical functions. But that image suggests an identifiable and fixed structure that is appropriate for each character and can be passed from one actor to another. More properly the text is an elixir which has to be 'taken internally' in repeated doses, until it transforms consciousness and also physical being. Or the text may be said to 'programme' the actors according to each individual talent and so draw forth inimitable effects according to the particular constitution of every individual performer.

To gain a better understanding of what Shakespeare wrote, it is necessary to search out the qualities of his text as an actor would in rehearsal and performance, seeking the clues which lead interpreters to make the characters live upon the stage in so many various ways. This should be an eminently practical study, felt in the pulse as well as in the head, involving action as much as thought and speech, and activating an individual and idiosyncratic 'impulse of being'.

*   *   *

The way Shakespeare thought about individual beings may be seen most clearly in early writing where a leading character holds the stage and talks. Here Shakespeare's conception is especially free. So when Richard the Second returns from Ireland after Bolingbroke has raised an army to threaten his authority, he enters asking a simple question:

> RICHARD   Barkloughly Castle call they this at hand?
> AUMERLE   Yea, my lord. How brooks your Grace the air
> After your late tossing on the breaking seas?
> RICHARD   Needs must I like it well. I weep for joy
> To stand upon my kingdom once again.
> Dear earth, I do salute thee with my hand,
> Though rebels wound thee with their horses' hoofs.
> *(Richard II*, III.ii.1–7)

Richard's question starts strongly, but energy slips away as 'they' introduces a sense that the king is not at home. Or is he speaking only to show that he does know something? Is it possible that he has not investigated his whereabouts before coming ashore? Is he playing a game and talking for the sake of talking, to show he is not dispirited? Aumerle's answer is in three short syllables, and then he changes the subject with a question of his own. To that Richard's reply is brief, colloquial, and firm; but may also be ironic, because a king is acknowledging necessity. Then a crux occurs in the text, because Richard's next words can imply that he has been weeping all the time, or that he starts weeping as he answers, or that he wills himself to weep or to act as if he were weeping. And the word 'joy' is another crux: does this mean that he is joyful, or is he covering up a deeper despair? Next the actor will have to decide whether he stoops (after 'stand') to touch the 'earth', and if so, how does he do so: 'salute' could be a formal gesture, but 'Dear earth' suggests something more intimate. Or possibly his action is wholly instinctive, and the movements quick and surprising. Certainly this is the moment when Richard voices thoughts that he had repressed earlier. The image he uses is violent, evoking the sound of galloping horses and a close-focused view of their hooves in unstoppable charge; the word 'wound', in the context of the play's action, indicates that the horses are preparing for battle.[13] The line ending with 'horses' hoofs' provides the strongest rhythm of the passage so far. The active and aggressive verb, 'wound', is placed strongly on the second accented syllable of the iambic line; it is perhaps the most emphatic word so far.

This short speech is sufficient to show how actively and openly Shakespeare was aware of his characters as he wrote, new impulses crowding one after another, represented by vocabulary, syntax, rhythm, sound, metre, gestures, silence, weeping. So the consciousness he has given to Richard is not static, but ranges forward and backward in time, considers both known and unknown circumstances, and is not wholly under control. The author seems to have been present within the mind and body of Richard, and hyper-alert, keenly inventive, ambitious to represent a full range of actions and reactions.

The actor has many decisions to make. All five of Richard's lines could carry self-wounding irony, so that his movement from thought to thought would be deliberately shocking. Or Richard may be speaking to protect himself from self-doubt and fear, or to create a more assured public performance. Or each transition in his thought might be instinctive, and when he addresses the earth he might take refuge in his own thoughts and isolate himself from those who wait on him. Played for maximum variety in this way, the king would seem like a rudderless vessel upon a swelling and breaking sea of feelings. (Aumerle's change of subject in line 2 may imply that the king had already lost interest in the castle before he could be answered, even this briefly.) What all readings would have in common is a strong dynamic, and a physical as well as vocal performance: the changes in the subject and direction of thought, and the varying lengths of the sentences

– the separate moves in the game of consciousness – can only be played in such a way.

Now the king's mind changes speed and reach yet again, as he starts a more reflective and balanced simile. But, before he speaks, both hands have probably touched the earth; and certainly tears and smiles have been seen, or at least imagined, on the king's face. Tenderness and domesticity replace the wounding hooves:

> As a long-parted mother with her child
> Plays fondly with her tears and smiles in meeting,
> So weeping-smiling greet I thee, my earth,
> And do thee favours with my royal hands.

After two sustained lines, in which the sense of Richard's words needs the full length of both, the rhythms change in a line that must have three or four separate units to make any sense at all. On 'weeping-smiling', Richard's speech may be overcome with emotion; or he may struggle to create the compound means to master and control his feeling by the act of speaking, in which case the last line could be self-critical, emphasised by stopping whatever gestures his hands are making. All four lines originate in the same single thought, and so they could be spoken on a single breath; if this is the case, a sense of an inward calm, or controlled emotion, would derive from that physical fact. However unruly Richard's thoughts, he has reached a more composed equilibrium, and it is from this that his next, more sustained sentence will gather its undoubted power:

> Feed not thy sovereign's foe, my gentle earth,
> Nor with thy sweets comfort his ravenous sense;
> But let thy spiders, that suck up thy venom,
> And heavy-gaited toads, lie in their way,
> Doing annoyance to the treacherous feet
> Which with usurping steps do trample thee;
> Yield stinging nettles to mine enemies;
> And when they from thy bosom pluck a flower,
> Guard it, I pray thee, with a lurking adder,
> Whose double tongue may with a mortal touch
> Throw death upon thy sovereign's enemies.

Throughout this sequence of thoughts, a tension exists between 'gentle earth' and 'sovereign's enemies'. The small scale of the earth's means of 'annoyance' contrasts with what is 'ravenous', 'treacherous', 'usurping', and with the trampling and plucking sensations deriving from the king's foes. Yet the 'lurking' adder sustains the thought which brings the long sentence to its firm conclusion. 'Throw death' can mean simply 'inflict death', but in association with 'pluck', 'guard', 'touch' it would be hard to banish a more active and practical sense as well, however strange and disproportionate. The adder's 'double tongue' introduces a further sense of word-play, as does 'guard' in its two senses of 'protect' and 'embellish or decorate'. There are other odd features – 'heavy-gaited toads' and the idea of soldiers picking a flower as if from the 'bosom' of a woman – so that a question arises as to whether performance should give an impression of hectic, self-mocking absurdity, or of complicated childishness.

In these lines another of Shakespeare's qualities as a writer has come into play: his mind is able to sustain a single line of thought and yet draw upon a consciousness at once sensitive and far-reaching, not losing contact with fugitive and half-formed sensations, or with practical actions.

Certainly this sequence of thought has now been played out, because Richard turns away from the earth to address the attendant lords. He acknowledges that he has been talking to inanimate objects and also using absurd verbal means ('senseless' implies both); and in effect he makes excuses for his own faltering response:

> Mock not my senseless conjuration, lords.
> This earth shall have a feeling, and these stones
> Prove armed soldiers, ere her native king
> Shall falter under foul rebellion's arms.

However strongly the earth is promised feeling and the stones endowed with aggressive might, the effect is weak and not strong, fearful and not brave. The response of the Bishop of Carlisle shows that in his view self-doubt is what Richard has most strongly expressed:

> Fear not, my lord; that power that made you king
> Hath power to keep you king in spite of all.
>
> (ll. 27–8)

Shakespeare's conception of Richard is of a man at war within himself, capable of both quick emotion and conscious effort, often in conflict with each other. He talks to communicate, but also to keep certain thoughts at bay and to encourage others. By speaking he is led to recognise thoughts that had earlier been unconscious or at least unregistered and undefined. Breath, phrasing, emphasis, as well as choice of words and images, are used to express and to betray the movements of the speaker's mind. And all the time speech is related to physical reality and actions, so that words are never the total statement. Nor does conscious will command totally the progress of the speaker: thoughts prepare for words, which in turn modify thoughts; and thoughts continue in the wake of speech, bringing new ideas and new needs to the surface of consciousness.

Such a passage, for all its precise images and metrical control, can be performed in many ways, with differing emphasis and implications but, if all the words are spoken so that consecutive sense is achieved, the shape of the speaker's experience will necessarily have to be coherent in performance. At this level of inward experience, however strongly or lightly it is indicated, Shakespeare's hold on the drama's action is firm and his imagination assured.

If Richard has knelt to salute the earth, nothing in the words will tell the actor when he should rise. If he has both wept and smiled, nothing dictates when this should cease. But he is sufficiently roused to think of 'armed soldiers' fighting on his behalf and, although two of the last three lines have a mid-line break in phrasing, 'native king' is firmly placed and the concluding phrase runs to full length. Perhaps Richard now stands in command; but 'falter' then will carry different associations, and the fourth syllable of that line will not be sufficiently stressed to hold firm emphasis. The king's mind cannot be wholly assured. Carlisle's argument for immediate practical action is left unanswered, so that Aumerle, the much younger man, interposes to explain what he thinks the king meant, countering the effect of his inaction (perhaps he cannot see the crack in the royal glass):

> He means, my lord, that we are too remiss;
> Whilst Bolingbroke, through our security,
> Grows strong and great in substance and in power.
>
> (ll. 33–5)

Now Richard does respond and fixes attention upon Aumerle, leading with a word that had more established meanings in Shakespeare's day than it has now: 'Discomfortable cousin! know'st thou not . . .'. He sees that this counsellor is distressed or causes distress in others: Aumerle lacks courage, and the four-syllable word, linked in sound with 'cousin', holds attention upon him lightly but persistently.

Richard's and Aumerle's eyes must surely meet here, since it is from this moment that the king launches upon a sustained image of kingship, as if spurred forward by Aumerle's fear rather than his own. For eighteen lines Richard is in charge:

> Discomfortable cousin! know'st thou not
> That when the searching eye of heaven is hid
> Behind the globe and lights the lower world

– the 'eye' of heaven may rise to the mind because the two men have just faced each other –

> Then thieves and robbers range abroad unseen
> In murders and in outrage boldly here;
> But when from under this terrestrial ball
> He fires the proud tops of the eastern pines
> And darts his light through every guilty hole,
> The murders, treasons, and detested sins,
> The cloak of night being pluck'd from off their backs,
> Stand bare and naked, trembling at themselves?
> So when this thief, this traitor, Bolingbroke,
> Who all this while hath revell'd in the night,
> Whilst we were wand'ring with the Antipodes,
> Shall see us rising in our throne, the east,
> His treasons will sit blushing in his face,
> Not able to endure the sight of day,
> But self-affrighted tremble at his sin.
>
> (ll. 36–53)

Thought polarises in this passage, the heavenly, royal, and global opposed to a blushing and, most affectingly, a trembling nakedness. Controlled strength and wild violence are interweaved, while ranging, revelling and wandering are opposed to 'fires', 'darts' and 'rising'. To speak this extended passage the actor has to control his breathing and so regularise his pulse to some extent – and the line-length phrasing reinforces this sense of control – so that the king's presence, verbal resource, and breath itself will alike hold attention by an innate authority.

How much Richard maintains contact with Aumerle depends on the relationship that the two actors have developed in their roles by this stage of the play, but whatever is achieved can be given strength if Aumerle is seen to accept progressively the new authority of his cousin king. Effortlessly it seems – the phrasing is untroubled now – Richard moves on to claim heavenly power. No one interposes, although what he says denies the need for action which has been urged by both advisers:

> Not all the water in the rough rude sea
> Can wash the balm off from an anointed king;
> The breath of worldly men cannot depose
> The deputy elected by the Lord.
> For every man that Bolingbroke hath press'd
> To lift shrewd steel against our golden crown,
> God for his Richard hath in heavenly pay
> A glorious angel. Then, if angels fight,
> Weak men must fall; for heaven still guards the right.

The 'rough rude sea' lacks the particularity of his earlier thoughts about Bolingbroke, but it is an overwhelmingly large image for Richard's adversary. Although this part of the speech starts with a negative, its depersonalised re-statement of a king's authority carries much greater assurance than Richard had achieved earlier. Rhythms falter only towards the close when 'Weak men' may indicate a return to the image used twice before of man in trembling nakedness, but nevertheless Richard can turn with buoyant courage to the Earl of Salisbury who now enters. Shakespeare has used words to effect a transformation in Richard's physical bearing.

On his entry Salisbury reports that all the Welsh recruits they had expected:

> ... hearing thou wert dead,
> Are gone to Bolingbroke, dispers'd, and fled.
>   (ll. 73–4)

The news is devastating and Shakespeare has arranged that it is told so that an audience sees that Richard, having composed his spoken thoughts, is wholly defenceless. He can only look pale until – once more – the young Aumerle has spoken, and then the young cousin's puzzled concern serves to release the king's deep despair. 'Angels' had not truly fortified his courage; they could not 'fight' in his mind with the same power as ordinary but very palpable men:

AUMERLE Comfort, my liege, why looks your Grace so pale?
RICHARD But now the blood of twenty thousand men
　　　　　Did triumph in my face, and they are fled;
　　　　　And, till so much blood thither come again,
　　　　　Have I not reason to look pale and dead?

Richard's words completely deny his earlier courage and when no one answers he proceeds to assert command only to move further towards despair, anticipating his own later flight from Bolingbroke's growing power:

All souls that will be safe, fly from my side;
For Time hath set a blot upon my pride.
　　　　　　　　　　　　　　　　　(ll. 80–1)

Shakespeare's view of Richard is of a man who never speaks the whole truth. Contact with other men is vital to his thought and assurance, and in their presence he will lie to give himself a semblance of strength and assurance. Then he retreats from speech into new or newly recognised thoughts, reaching out to gather concepts or images from his past, his environment, and his own immediate experience. He is caught by his own words; he struggles within their restraints and suggestions, until he tries to pin down the source of his insecurity. At last he blames his 'pride', but this does not satisfy him, because a moment later he scornfully repudiates the thought: 'I had forgot myself; am I not King?' (1. 83).

Richard II is often called the most verbal and, in a literary sense, the most poetic of Shakespeare's plays, but this short episode calls for actions, varying breath control, silences, and changing focus of attention. When his speech has greatest confidence, Richard has soon to turn 'pale and dead' and does not speak until his young cousin appeals to him.

*   *   *

Of course words are not uttered by the brain alone, but depend also on breath and movements in the mouth and throat, and they are modified by bearing, posture, and physical action. This is true in the performance of any play, but Shakespeare's awareness of the sensations associated with words and of the nature of the speech-act itself meant that his dialogue uses to unusual effect this necessary conjunction of thought, speech, and body. His characters were not disembodied in his creative mind; the very breathing which makes it possible to utter words can represent the nature of a speaker with as much clarity as glittering, resonant, persuasive, or simple words.

Shakespeare seems to have been constantly aware of the physical component of speech. In *The Rape of Lucrece* (1593–4), he specified, in his own person as narrator, a number of occasions when words had to give place to silence:

> Lo, here, the hopeless merchant of this loss,
> With head declin'd and voice damm'd up with woe,
> With sad-set eyes and wretched arms across,
> From lips new-waxen pale begins to blow
> The grief away that stops his answer so;
>> But wretched as he is he strives in vain;
>> What he breathes out his breath drinks up again.
>
> (ll. 1660–6)

A still more physical and almost comic image describes Collatine's conflict between sorrow and pride – a conflict similar to that experienced by King Richard:

> As through an arch the violent roaring tide
> Outruns the eye that doth behold his haste,
> Yet in the eddy boundeth in his pride
> Back to the strait that forc'd him on so fast,
> In rage sent out, recall'd in rage, being past;
>> Even so his sighs, his sorrows, make a saw,
>> To push grief on, and back the same grief draw.
>
> (ll. 1667–73)

When Collatine is at last able to speak, the words come indistinctly:

The deep vexation of his inward soul
Hath serv'd a dumb arrest upon his tongue;
Who, mad that sorrow should his use control,
Or keep him from heart-easing words so long,
Begins to talk; but through his lips do throng
   Weak words, so thick come, in his poor heart's aid,
   That no man could distinguish what he said.
(ll. 1779–85)

In the previous chapter an interview between King John and
Hubert, in which the servant is persuaded to kill Prince Arthur,
was used to show Shakespeare's use of words as signs between
the two men; comprehension of certain very specific words was
the test for mutual understanding. But in Shakespeare's mind words
did not hold all the drama; in a later scene John reveals that these
signs were not the whole experience:

Hadst thou but shook thy head or made a pause,
When I spake darkly what I purposed,
Or turn'd an eye of doubt upon my face,
As bid me tell my tale in express words,
Deep shame had struck me dumb, made me break off,
And those thy fears might have wrought fears in me.
But thou didst understand me by my signs,
And didst in signs again parley with sin;
Yea, without stop, didst let thy heart consent,
And consequently thy rude hand to act
The deed which both our tongues held vile to name.
Out of my sight, and never see me more!
(IV.ii.231–42)

The persons whom Shakespeare imagined are complete beings
and not talking heads: the manner of their speaking and their
unspoken thoughts are also part of the meaning of the scene.

Shakespeare's pleasure in words gave him the ability to work
in this way. In his mind words had a restless life, prompting
awareness to reach beyond earlier limitations, awakening memories from other situations, leading thought to outstrip thought
and to find or create further words. Words themselves changed
in value as they were spoken and according to whom they were
spoken. They overreached intention, leaping out into new meanings

or into nonsense. They were sensational in that they awakened his senses in a more than pictorial manner, carrying an impression of physical action, hearing, touch, taste, balance, instability, speed. For Shakespeare the use of words was part of being alive and, when writing his plays, he was able to adapt his own consciousness to the predicament of each person involved in the action. He lived anew in his mind through them, so that the words he gave them seem to spring from independent intelligences both conscious and unconscious, giving to each character a private centre and distinctive energy. Actors are set a course to run which is laid down in the words which Shakespeare has given them, a trial of their skills and innate strengths, as they 'find the characters' and give them new life in mental and physical particulars.

For readers and critics this way of working has immense consequences. They cannot be content with a response to the words on the page which is defined only by the use of other words. Like the actors and author, they need to bring to the text a sense of the 'impulse of being', of lived experience, palpable, idiosyncratic, conscious and unconscious. They have to gain a sense of the multiple and actual experiences implicit in what Shakespeare wrote. This goes far beyond the usual understanding of 'character' in either play or novel, and beyond usual perceptions of individual character in life.

4

Characters

The animation of the character of Richard the Second for a hundred lines or so, in word and deed, spoken and unspoken thought, impulse, deep feeling, and deliberate choice, exemplifies Shakespeare's basic means of setting the plays in action. But no more than that. From the first, he continued to experiment constantly and showed a seemingly endless interest in how persons presented themselves and were revealed without their knowledge. He must have watched actors closely, as well as persons in real life, and studied with great care all the complicated processes of speech. There was no scope in his manuscripts for long descriptive stage-directions about behaviour or intention, and he could not know whether his original punctuation would be preserved in the 'parts' which were written out by playhouse scriveners for use by the actors. He therefore had to learn how to orchestrate speech and performance solely by the words set down to be spoken, with the help of few and minimal directions, which might or might not survive unaltered into a promptbook or other copies. Such conditions did not daunt him; they seem, rather, to have stimulated new endeavours and refined his ways of using words.

Sometimes we may sense that Shakespeare set himself problems. A few years after writing *Richard the Second*, for example, he set about showing how two persons come very slowly to accept each other's love. The first meeting of Benedick and Beatrice in *Much Ado About Nothing* could not be like the quick-fire exchange of Romeo and Juliet's encounter as they step out of the festivities to be alone. Shakespeare now used a public occasion when the couple are watched by relatives, friends, and numerous attendants. The mutual acknowledgement of their love comes much later, after each one has privately recognised the possibility of attraction to the other. Even then Shakespeare chose to delay mutual confidence until both persons had been deeply involved in talk about other things than their passions, and then to delay still more the moment when they kiss. The result is delicate and dramatic, with a sense of powerful feelings held in reserve until restraint is no longer possible. In performance the scene in which they confess their mutual love can oscillate between being very funny and painfully serious.

In the third Act of *The Merchant of Venice* Bassanio will win Portia as his bride if he chooses the correct casket out of three. Here Shakespeare set himself to tell a story in which this condition has been set up by the lady's father in his will, to which she has agreed. The first decision he made, after providing a preliminary dialogue, was to set the two characters at a distance from each other, so that their feelings could be expressed with the least disturbance from each other's presence. Portia knows at once when Bassanio has chosen rightly, because she has witnessed other suitors fail with the other two caskets; and so her thoughts rush onwards in happiness, well before his. Yet she also glances mentally backwards to what is more comprehensible. Then at the last moment, her mind hurries forward with exclamation and repetition, towards the realisation of a new fear:

> How all the other passions fleet to air,
> As doubtful thoughts, and rash-embrac'd despair,
> And shudd'ring fear, and green-ey'd jealousy!
> O love, be moderate, allay thy ecstasy,
> In measure rain thy joy, scant this excess!
> I feel to much thy blessing. Make it less,
> For fear I surfeit.
>
> (III.ii.108–14)

High-pitched joy sustains this speech, but that emotion is not itself expressed directly. Instead, Portia names her other passions and begs for some reduction of her happiness. But while her ecstasy is largely unspoken, it is thrillingly present in the movement and shape of her thoughts, her breathing, rhythms, and very being.

When Bassanio finds a picture of Portia inside the lead casket and so learns that he has won his bride, he fixes his thoughts upon this reflection of Portia rather than on the reality of her actual person standing at a little distance. He also avoids direct expression of feeling, persisting in a consideration of the skill and of the man who painted the portrait. But his state of mind is also expressed in *how* he speaks – the brevity of his exclamations and questions, and the rapidity of his counter-thoughts:

What find I here?
Fair Portia's counterfeit! What demi-god
Hath come so near creation? Move these eyes?
Or whether riding on the balls of mine
Seem they in motion? Here are sever'd lips
Parted with sugar breath; so sweet a bar
Should sunder such sweet friends. Here in her hairs
The painter plays the spider, and hath woven
A golden mesh t'entrap the hearts of men
Faster than gnats in cobwebs. But her eyes –
How could he see to do them? Having made one,
Methinks it should have power to steal both his,
And leave itself unfurnish'd. Yet look how far
The substance of my praise doth wrong this shadow
In underprizing it, so far this shadow
Doth limp behind the substance. Here's the scroll,
The continent and summary of my fortune.

(ll. 114–30)

Whereas Portia sought control over her emotions, Bassanio holds them at a distance, working swiftly to cope with a more unexpected experience. He relates what is almost beyond comprehension with what is tangible, his wholly new imaginative and sexual experience with a physical and inanimate reality that he is more able to grasp. Although he fixes his thoughts on the mere picture of Portia, images of estrangement, entrapment, insignificance, poverty, incapacity, and abundant wealth all come insistently into his mind; so too, does friendship – the relationship of 'such sweet friends', like that which had prompted Antonio's loan, without which he could not have been a suitor to Portia – and thoughts of loss and wrongdoing, of the falseness of words, and of pain and legal documents. In less excited moments all these ideas would have made him pause and remember the shadowy nature of his bold and 'prized' appearance as a wealthy and independent suitor. Perhaps he turns to the scroll with some earnestness: at any rate, he does not turn yet to speak to Portia, and she remains silent.

By these means Shakespeare was able to suggest a 'subtext', a consciousness not directly expressed in words, which the actor must create in performance if the words are to be lifelike or true in their context. Without a strong subtextual insecurity Bassanio would seem perverse, an impertinent critic of an art-object, rather than someone in love with a person who is standing no further away than the other side of the stage. When at last he approaches Portia, having read the scroll, he does acknowledge his unmanageable confusion. He is now almost formal in bearing, as if his mind has to be very careful in coming to terms with his good fortune. He starts simply, politely, and gently, before trying to explain his delay and uncertainties:

> A gentle scroll. Fair lady, by your leave;
> I come by note, to give and to receive.
> Like one of two contending in a prize,
> That thinks he hath done well in people's eyes,
> Hearing applause and universal shout,
> Giddy in spirit, still gazing in a doubt
> Whether those peals of praise be his or no;
> So, thrice-fair lady, stand I even so,
> As doubtful whether what I see be true,
> Until confirm'd, sign'd ratified by you.
>
> (ll. 139–48)

So his words do at last flow, but still unsteadily; this is not a time of peaceful joy, when he might confess 'I were but little happy if I could say how much.'[1]

The abundant vitality with which Shakespeare used words was joined with a scepticism about their power as signifiers of human beings: words are wanton and not in the last resort to be trusted. We have to reach beyond words, or rather *through* them, to grasp at the nature of these characters. Sometimes a subtext will suggest meanings that seem beyond the concious reach of the speaker, as if a sense of consequence or compulsion lies within the unconscious mind. So Portia replies to Bassanio by first picking up his word 'stand' and so placing herself in a balance with him, but then she is suddenly apprehensive about her own value:

> You see me, Lord Bassanio, where I stand,
> Such as I am. . . .
>
> (III.ii.149–50)

She seems to pick up 'underprizing' from Bassanio earlier speech, and his 'continent and summary of my fortune' (ll. 128 and 130), for she plays with these ideas of business-like proceedings rather than speaking of generous love – until apprehension or modesty takes hold of her as well, vying with her happiness. On the one hand, with 'happy', 'happier', and 'happiest', her speech expresses 'ecstasy' and 'joy' (ll. 111 and 112), but on the other hand she is concerned about the as yet unknown meeting when her virginal sense of self-possession will be converted into 'something' other.

Perhaps Portia is conscious of all the sexual imagery in her speech, and of its drive towards a climax and then its yielding which with rhythm and sound accentuate this. But she can hardly be fully conscious, when she gives her ring to Bassanio, of further implications in her words of a strong possessive instinct. (Only at the end of the play, with a great show of pleasure, she will have the confidence to 'exclaim' (at l. 175) on Bassanio for breaking his promise, and he will have to accept her rule over events.) Yet even now she may sense something of a reversal of power which will have to be acted out, knowing instinctively that her commitment of all she is to her husband is not going to be a passive subjection to him. At least, she keeps a sense of humour, a knowledge that all this earnest exchange can come very close to being absurd:

You see me, Lord Bassanio, where I stand,
Such as I am. Though for myself alone
I would not be ambitious in my wish
To wish myself much better, yet for you
I would be trebled twenty times myself,
A thousand times more fair, ten thousand times more rich,
That only to stand high in your account,
I might in virtues, beauties, livings, friends,
Exceed account. But the full sum of me
Is sum of something which, to term in gross,
Is an unlesson'd girl, unschool'd, unpractis'd;
Happy in this, she is not yet so old
But she may learn; happier than this,
She is not bred so dull but she can learn;
Happiest of all is that her gentle spirit
Commits itself to yours to be directed,
As from her lord, her governor, her king.
Myself and what is mine to you and yours
Is now converted. But now I was the lord
Of this fair mansion, master of my servants,

Queen o'er myself; and even now, but now,
This house, these servants, and this same myself,
Are yours – my lord's. I give them with this ring,
Which when you part from, lose, or give away,
Let it presage the ruin of your love
And be my vantage to exclaim on you.

(III.ii.149–75)

How Portia speaks her last few lines of warning will depend very much on the person who performs the role, but through her words, from underneath the text, suggestions of challenge, self-sufficient authority, and pleasure in the exercise of power are almost sure to be heard. The rhythms, without help from the word-play, are sufficient to say as much. Portia does not speak the words of conventional obedience with ironic or rebellious intention, but rather with excitement, tenderness, sexual awareness, and authority. The shape and rhythms of the speech say something which is as real within Portia as the impulse to use the words she chooses. This less specified and less conscious involvement in the moment is perhaps what is most true to herself and to her sense of the man who stands before her.

She must have moved closer to Bassanio during this speech and that action is as much a part of what she wishes to express as the words she speaks. At first they had been standing at a distance to view each other, but now they are close enough for Portia to 'give' the ring into his hands. Bassanio has no words until she is quite finished and her ring is his, and then he can only acknowledge the gift with a rather stiff formality. He takes up Portia's challenge with an oath on his life:

Madam, you have bereft me of all words.
Only my blood speaks to you in my veins;
And there is such confusion in my powers
As, after some oration fairly spoke
By a beloved prince, there doth appear
Among the buzzing pleased multitude,
Where every something, being blent together,
Turns to a wild of nothing, save of joy
Express'd and not express'd. But when this ring
Parts from this finger, then parts life from hence;
O, then be bold to say Bassanio's dead!

(ll. 176–86)

Shakespeare has imagined these two characters as beings impelled by thoughts which words cannot express fully. Not only do words suggest a subtext, beneath their more obvious meanings in the speaker's minds, but it is on this unspoken level that the compatibility of the two persons depends. This deeper layer of meaning reaches beyond the present moment requiring later resolution.

Although this is a betrothal scene, the text does not indicate when the lovers kiss. The actors must choose the time for this, but it would be in keeping with Bassanio's expressed doubts about whether 'what I see be true' and with the ritual of an exchange of rings if the kiss were delayed until the very last words quoted here. They have now no more to say; kissing has become a comparatively easy option, and it is Nerissa and Gratiano who speak next, wishing 'good joy' to the couple. If the concluding kiss is delayed this long, the audience will have been kept waiting and so be the more likely to appreciate the self-regarding hesitations which are an instinctive part of this lovers' meeting.

Portia has much to say about her own character, but she does not say all; she is far more than 'an unlesson'd girl, unschool'd, unpractis'd'. In this she is like all Shakespeare's major characters: the speeches which seem to sum up their natures do not lead audiences very close to Shakespeare's conception. Richard the Second is not, simply, a person who 'wasted time' and is at last wasted by time.[2] Othello is not, simply, someone who 'lov'd not wisely, but too well', Lear a man 'more sinned against than sinning', Hamlet a 'coward' or a man compelled by 'madness'.[3] Nor is it truly because Benedick and Beatrice are 'too wise' that they cannot 'woo peaceably'.[4]

Even a play's action, the development of its plot, may not provide sufficient indication of what the characters are made of. When Gemma Jones was preparing to play Hermione in *The Winter's Tale* at Stratford-upon-Avon, she deduced from the story that the trial scene would call for 'real tears' and violent action; she and the director discussed how she could enter in manacles and dragged by her hair. But the speech directed otherwise. The actress soon learned that it is, very simply, 'too long' to be spoken emotively; it 'becomes self-pitying' that way:

> Her speech has a fluidity and simplicity compared to the more complex intellectual agility of the first scene, where she played with words. She is [now] articulate, objective and strong, because

she is right. She is innocent and she knows it. She does not have to plead her cause or prove that she is true. She has faith.[5]

In consequence, Gemma Jones spent hours of rehearsal 'discovering and caring for the nuances of meaning in Hermione's speech to the court, and the delicate balance of a stress that can illuminate or confuse'.[6] Truth of character lies neither in plot nor in verbal definition, but deep within the words Shakespeare used, in what they do not say or what they only hint at, and sometimes in their very sound and movement.

Macbeth's reaction to his first meeting with the witches illustrates these techniques in an unusual way because Banquo, Ross, and Angus stand at some distance and their reactions and comments mark the physical and silent elements of the central performance:

MACBETH   Two truths are told,
  As happy prologues to the swelling act
  Of the imperial theme. – I thank you, gentlemen. –
  This supernatural soliciting
  Cannot be ill; cannot be good. – If ill,
  Why hath it given me earnest of success,
  Commencing in a truth? I am Thane of Cawdor.
  If good, why do I yield to that suggestion
  Whose horrid image doth unfix my hair,
  And make my seated heart knock at my ribs,
  Against the use of nature? Present fears
  Are less than horrible imaginings.
  My thought, whose murder yet is but fantastical,
  Shakes so my single state of man
  That function is smother'd in surmise,
  And nothing is, but what is not.
BANQUO   Look, how our partner's rapt.
MACBETH   If Chance will have me King, why, Chance may crown
      me
  Without my stir.
BANQUO   New honours come upon him,
  Like our strange garments, cleave not to their mould,
  But with the aid of use.
MACBETH   Come what come may,
  Time and the hour runs through the roughest day.
BANQUO   Worthy Macbeth, we stay upon your leisure.

MACBETH   Give me your favour; my dull brain was wrought
   With things forgotten. . . .

(I.iii.127–50)

Macbeth here speaks first of his own physical reactions and is aware that he is under observation; in this his words are directly expressive of his mental state, joining with the 'swelling' under-tow of royal thoughts, inner suffering, insecurity, and loneliness. Antithetical statements tighten and relax their hold, either way cleaving to his present experience. They also show that he senses now, at some deep level, a connection with his first words in the scene – 'So foul and fair a day I have not seen' (l. 38): 'nothing is, but what is not' he says, and then is 'rapt' in thought and silent. Still more mysteriously, these few words echo the witches' incantations heard by the audience long before his approach, at the very beginning of the play itself:

– When shall we three meet again?
   In thunder, lightning, or in rain?
– When the hurlyburly's done,
   When the battle's lost and won. . . .
– Fair is foul, and foul is fair:
   Hover through the fog and filthy air.
(I.i.1–11)

Macbeth does not accept easily, as the witches have done, that ill is good, or fair foul. (Is he responding to their supernatural suggestions, powerful, though no longer spoken? Some in the audience might think so.) He wrestles his way forward through questions and assertions, and knows that his instinctive physical response is opposed to his conscious and thriving thought. Even when words seem to provide a release from torment – 'Chance may crown me Without my stir' – he is still unable to move or speak further. There is time for Banquo to comment on how his thoughts of honour do not 'cleave . . . to their mould' – an image suggesting deep-set struggle and pain. The couplet with which Macbeth speaks again after this silence, and which provides the verbal conclusion of his soliloquy, is so light in rhythm that he seems evasive as he attempts to generalise:

> Come what come may,
> Time and the hour runs through the roughest day.

Even now Macbeth remains isolated and his thoughts unresolved; he has to be urged to join the others. Then he manages, haltingly, to break free from unspoken thoughts, at least in almost all of what he says.

*   *   *

Shakespeare is so famous for creating life-like characters that an important distinction may be forgotten. These 'characters' (as we have come to call them, although the word was not used in this way until towards the end of the seventeenth century) are *not* like persons in real life. No one we know will speak like this, be so decisive, economical, and interesting. No one actually lives with such vivid intensity. Shakespeare's characters have only the appearance of reality. It is the movement of thought and feeling implicit in the words of the text, the underlying physical awareness, emotional strength, and eagerness of mind which give a semblance of actual persons. If these characters could be transported off stage, they would founder immediately; they would need a new supply of Shakespeare's words or a less vital engagement.

On stage they are more than life-like; they seem substantial, as if they could exist outside the bounds of the drama. The Nurse in *Romeo and Juliet* is an early example of this quality, achieved by a great range and richness of allusion. In reminiscences and digressions her life-story and a daily routine seem to be laid out for inspection. But her unwieldy body, slow breath, day-dreams and memories, her need to fasten on certain words and phrases to keep her thoughts in some order, her egotism, and her absorption in Juliet, all this is also established, by the way was it were, in speeches which arise naturally from the plot and action. When Paris is suggested as Juliet's bridegroom, for example, the Nurse's response is large-hearted, soft and acquiescent, and at the same time emphatic:

> A man, young lady! lady, such a man
> As all the world – why, he's a man of wax.
> (I.iii.76–7)

Her last word here is not to be understood easily: the verb to 'wax' is to grow (and Shakespeare used it in this sense elsewhere in a similar context[7]); but 'wax' is a very yielding substance; and, thirdly, perfect models and elaborate toys were, at this time, made 'of wax'. The possibility that all these suggestions are involved here does not argue, as it might in life, that the Nurse has a highly subtle mind; she seems, rather, to be muddled as well as emphatic, grabbing at a word which is more revealing than she intends, showing an unthinking and physically responsive intuition, rather than intellectual acuity. The rhythms of the two verse-lines, their repetitions and incomplete phrases, the exclamations and climactic position of the crucial monosyllable, all combine to enhance the impression of a very particular mind in heightened and confused operation. An actress might well select just one of *wax*'s possible meanings and so give her own sense of the Nurse's character, but alternative implications may nevertheless resonate in the minds of her audience, which may be alerted by the responses of other characters on stage who are impatient of her nature and so re-interpret her intentions.

In the same play, a bitter, sensuous, and aggressive mind is presented with comparable economy and richness. Like the Nurse's reminiscences, Mercutio's invocation of Queen Mab in Act I, scene iv, serves to establish and display the range of an idiosyncratic imagination. But then his talk with other characters has a more secret energy, whether in mockery of the Nurse or in preparing to fight, or in realising that he is indeed killed. A self-wounding sense of self seems to feed on its own perceptions, even while reaching out for understanding. So Mercutio challenges Tybalt, after Romeo has refused to fight:

MERCUTIO Tybalt, you rat-catcher, will you walk?
TYBALT What wouldst thou have with me?
MERCUTIO Good King of Cats, nothing but one of your nine
  lives; that I mean to make bold withal, and, as you shall use
  me hereafter, dry-beat the rest of the eight. Will you pluck
  your sword out of his pilcher by the ears? Make haste, lest
  mine be about your ears ere it be out. (III.i.73ff)

'Good King of Cats' outpaces Mercutio's first word-play with Tybalt's name – it is the cat's name in the fable of Reynard the Fox – and so mocks Tybalt for giving attention and himself for getting involved. 'Make bold' is everyday talk not appropriate to duelling, and so are the threat of cudgelling ('dry-beat') and the hackneyed politeness of 'as you shall use me'. Mercutio pretends that Tybalt's sword is reluctant to leave its leather protection or 'pilcher' by endowing it with life of its own as distinct from Tybalt's (see 'by the ears'). This grotesque image is then transferred to his own sword, as if it were about to start the dry-beating on its own account: to fight 'by the ears' was ordinarily used of angry dogs, cats, and other animals, and to be 'about the ears' was to brawl in a manner far from the finesse of a duellist with 'the immortal passado, the punto reverso' and the other niceties with which Mercutio had associated with Tybalt in his absence.[8] Mercutio has said that he fights to prove his honour (see 'O calm, dishonour-able, vile submission', l. 71), but these subsequent words imply that he engages now in a senseless brawl. He grows strong with mockery of his opponent, and also of himself; as he draws his sword he denigrates his own action. Laughter mingles with pas-sion and excitement, and possibly with fear or self-doubt. The words are simple, but the state of mind very complex. The actor need not realise exactly all that seems to be happening inside Mercutio's mind, but as the two duellists draw swords and be-come absolutely alert, the audience's attention will be alert too and both actors' involvement finely tuned.

Sometimes Shakespeare gives the audience a far clearer view of a speaker's thoughts than that possessed by the character at any level of consciousness. Such a moment is Benedick's solilo-quy in *Much Ado About Nothing*, after he has been tricked into believing that Beatrice pines in love for him. The audience has laughed freely as the conspirators laid the bait, but Benedick's first words betray no sense of these absurdities:

This can be no trick: the conference was sadly borne; they have the truth of this from Hero; they seem to pity the lady; it seems her affections have their full bent. Love me! Why, it must be requited. I hear how I am censur'd: they say I will bear myself proudly if I perceive the love come from her; they say, too, that she will rather die than give any sign of affection. I did never think to marry. I must not seem proud; happy are they that hear their detractions and can put them to mending. They say the lady is fair; 'tis a truth, I can bear them witness; and virtuous; 'tis so, I cannot reprove it; and wise, but for loving me. By my troth, it is no addition to her wit; nor no great argument of her folly, for I will be horribly in love with her. I may chance have some odd quirks and remnants of wit broken on me because I have railed so long against marriage; but doth not the appetite alter? A man loves the meat in his youth that he cannot endure in his age. Shall quips, and sentences, and these paper bullets of the brain, awe a man from the career of his humour? No; the world must be peopled. When I said I would die a bachelor, I did not think I should live till I were married. Here comes Beatrice. By this day, she's a fair lady; I do spy some marks of love in her. (II.iii.201ff)

The more emphatically Benedick says 'This can be no trick', the more the audience will laugh, because in no way was 'the conference . . . sadly borne': already the audience knows that Benedick's good sense has deserted him. From 'Why, it must be requited' onwards, they are ahead of his prevarications. They know that he tries to save his own dignity by overreaching criticism – 'I will be horribly in love with her' – and to justify his capitulation by irrelevant cliché – 'the world must be peopled'. The phrasing and rhythms lengthen as he becomes more accustomed to his new self, but all this is stilled when Beatrice enters, her words thoroughly ill-suited to his expectation: 'Against my will I am sent to bid you come in to dinner.' Benedick cannot sense how far this is from his expectation, whereas the audience might almost expect his words as he prepares to meet her: 'I do spy some marks of love in her.' While 'spy' continues an assumption of superior intelligence, Benedick cannot understand how inapposite his words are, or how busy and self-deceived his imagination. The audience laughs at a joke which the witty Benedick is unable see.

*   *   *

It is not surprising that Paul Scofield was impatient with the scholar who told him to play a symbol or represent an idea. The very opposite course of action, which seeks to give definition to a performance by inventing a detailed pre-history or using far-off memories of real-life people, even if these are irrelevant or distracting, would be a more effective way of making Shakespeare's lines come alive on stage. The plays were written with a keen awareness of 'psychological processes that ordinarily precede or determine human action'. That was how Shakespeare imagined the beings which he called into existence to take part in his plays. They were not composed and static portraits. They were not primarily representations of forces within society, or within persons or history. The texts of the plays invite actors to realise these characters as conscious minds, capable of thought and feelings on several levels and at differing speeds, and inhabiting whole human beings, bodies as well as minds.

Some writers for the stage are not aware of the physical accompaniments of speech – pulse-rate, breathing, change of attention, bodily tensions – and so provide difficult, confusing, and often irrelevant problems for the speakers of their dialogue. But Shakespeare seems to have envisioned the complete *action* which is speech, even as he was writing, being present, imaginatively, in his characters before they speak and as they speak. So it comes about that he always seems to stay ahead of actors in rehearsal, tempting them to explore further and deeper, and often goading them; and this explains why the technical problems of actors in his plays are at one with the problems of interpretation and the physical realisation of individual character. Words, for Shakespeare, were not signs or intellectual counters for manipulation, and his speeches not simply sequences of words, moves in a game of discourse. Words and speeches, poetry and argument, silence and action, were all part of an image of living reality. The persons he created for his plays breathe, move, look; they touch, listen, respond, stiffen and relax; and they reach out from the present moment into a future; they express themselves by silent actions and instinctive reactions, as well as by words. They are like human beings in real situations, but simpler and bolder; they have heightened awareness, contrasting rather than muddled emotions, quick intelligence even when slow in speech or action, and strong physical presences.

This invented world was designed to find its full life in performance on an open stage in the middle of an audience. However carefully Shakespeare tuned the verse or shaped a sentence, whatever half-conscious sensations were alive in his mind on behalf of his characters, the completed text had to await possession and fleshing out by the 'cry of players'; it was the pre-text for an engagement of living actors with his words, and with themselves and their audiences. The finished text had to be sufficiently resilient to survive and triumph in performance in such an arena and in such an embodiment.

One way of writing under these conditions would be to project oneself into the plays and manipulate the world on stage around that fixed centre. Christopher Marlowe, Shakespeare's exact contemporary, probably worked in that way, modifying and extending his own consciousness from play to play and so exploring the limits of his confidence and speculation. Numerous modern writers have come close to confessing that this is their preferred method. Accused of putting his own persona into his work, Tennessee Williams asked what else he could do:

> I mean the very root-necessity of all creative work is to express those things most involved in one's particular experience. Otherwise, is the work, however well executed, not manufactured, a synthetic thing?[9]

A central character who is a stand-in for the author is often discernible, as is plainly the case in Arthur Miller's *After the Fall*, Simon Gray's *Butley* and *Otherwise Engaged*, or Arnold Wesker's trilogy of plays based on his own family, beginning with *Chicken Soup with Barley*. Other dramatists seem to split themselves into two personas in their plays: the writer-brothers in Sam Shepard's *True West*, or the two poets in Harold Pinter's *No Man's Land*. Sometimes a different setting in time and place, with a change of profession or physical characteristics, may disguise the author's own presence, but not completely so; so the central character in Brecht's *Galileo*, who is responsible for most of the play's action and the force of its argument, is grounded in the author's own twentieth-century predicament and consciousness. But with Shakespeare's plays none of these equations work, except perhaps for brief moments only, notably in *Richard the Second*, *Henry the Fourth*, *As You Like It*, *Hamlet*, *King Lear* and *The Tempest*. These traces of the author's own voice are reminders of how completely the author's point of view has elsewhere given way to the initiative of imaginary beings.

None of Shakespeare's contemporaries had a similar facility. Ben Jonson banished himself from his major plays, but very seldom allowed any of his invented characters to function as if their independent, imagined beings were in control of words and actions; the masterplan is always dominant, even when threatened by the author's pleasure in his own inventions; and the author's style of writing is recognisable from character to character. Webster, Middleton, and Massinger invented a wide range of persons to serve the actions and arguments of their plays, but required them to carry a great load of their own observations on human behaviour at the cost of independent vitality. Sometimes their characters function like animals in a ring, going through the motions required to complete preordained patterns, rather than acting or speaking in their own time or making one choice out of many.

Comparisons with Shakespeare, both Elizabethan and modern, do less than justice to the other authors, because none can match his lack of self-absorption and endless versatility. He seems to have developed a unique way of working, in which he did truly make division of himself, his mind burning as brightly and independently in one part of an imagined world as in another. Perhaps the closest to achieving this are Aeschylus and Sophocles, but once their characters hold the stage they speak only for themselves and for the moment, confronting no more than one or two other characters, or the members of a chorus who are usually at some distance and do not share the same predicament. The characters of ancient tragedy are not called upon to provide a Shakespearian quickness of interplay with others or with a constantly changing situation (stichomythia has very strict constraints); originally they were realised before a huge audience, and they wore masks to simplify and strengthen what was actually achieved in performance.

*   *   *

In the 'quick forge' of his thought, fully engaged in his writing, Shakespeare did not reveal himself in any one part of it. His characters alone possess the stage and we must look behind them if we wish to observe how he worked and how best to respond to the text.

Firstly we may say that dramatic meaning never resides wholly in words, but rather in the being of the speaker – not merely the speaker's mind, but the whole engagement of that particular person in a particular situation. This is why Shakespeare's plays cannot be quoted without gross misrepresentation: the words themselves and alone, speak neither for Shakespeare nor for his characters.

The entire living actor speaking those words, among other actors and in the presence of an audience, is what they have been set down to provoke and to transmit, and only in that embodiment, different in every performance, do they function adequately.

Writing in this way, Shakespeare must have given full attention to his choice of words even while knowing that their effect would never be constant. If he ever thought about uttering 'the truth' about this subject or that, a definitive picture of a certain kind of person or of a particular social or political situation, he would have despaired of success. All he wrote in the plays was written to be charged and changed by his collaborators, a prey to luck and to time. He was meticulous as he wrote – to provide flexibility and strength requires absolute definition – but knew very well that what he controlled by words was there to be explored and extended, and sometimes contradicted, in performance. The fact that Shakespeare took little trouble to ensure authoritative publication of his plays (except when very imperfect texts had been issued without leave) should also warn us that he was not concerned with what can be deduced from the printed word alone.

A second conclusion to be drawn from his methods of writing and characterisation is that Shakespeare was interested in living realities more than in argument, statement, documentation, history, psychology, philosophy, or any kind of scholarly or critical thought. His view of the world was his sense of people living around him, and was grounded in human encounter and activity, not in theory or authority. It can be best known through the medium of theatre performance, not in any concept or verbal interpretation.

This is not to say that Shakespeare trusted deeds rather than words, because in his plays deeds often spring from words, and words are themselves part of human actions. But it does imply other attitudes. In a modern sense, he was a natural revolutionary, because the only way he could write a play was to set imaginary people in action together and let them actuate change, or allow events to change them.

In one sense, Shakespeare was not an intellectual, since intellectual comprehension was never his sole purpose and the statement of ideas had, in itself, little to offer. Nor was he a committed writer, in the sense that he believed in this or that formulation of the human predicament, political, moral, or philosophical. But he was committed in the sense that he strove to create images of living reality which held attention and could be carried to conclusions that were, in effect but not in statement, a clarification of earlier impressions.

A third conclusion is more obvious: he was not anti-intellectual. His thought was precise, practical, and sensuous: merely to explore the wealth of sensuous experience implicit in a speech of Richard the Second or Macbeth, or of any leading character in the plays, is to set an actor working to his uttermost, open to many sensations and drawing on his own life experience, as well as responding to the linguistic, musical, and technical brilliance of the text. The quickness of Shakespeare's mind will often awaken spontaneous laughter as his plays are rehearsed and as his words fulfil and go beyond expectations. The inescapable modification of what he had envisioned might have ensured bitter ironies – something of this can be seen in Ben Jonson's non-dramatic writings or in the words of many contemporary dramatists in interview – but to Shakespeare's abundantly active mind the unexpected probably provoked pleasure and, perhaps, inner laughter at himself and at others.

5

Interplay

If Shakespeare's characters are neither variations of himself, nor factors in some argument or parable, nor people determined by particular physical or psychological features, how can they be defined? One answer would be to say that their 'characters' depend on the words they choose, their affective imagery and field of reference, their patterns of thought as presented in syntax, rhythm, metre, rhetorical structure. Thought-processes show the individual energies of mind and suggest a physical involvement in the moment by moment concerns of the drama. To know the characters they play, actors must be patient and search out the smallest cues and wait for inspiration or intuition, or happy accident, to give a sense that they are on, what is for them, the correct track. However, this answer still leaves a great deal unexplained.

What was Shakespeare's way of choosing a character, or of inventing or finding a character? How does one differ essentially from another? What kind of certainty does an actor find in his or her role, and can one interpretation be more right than another? To all these enquiries, a single answer must serve for the moment, because they all involve wider issues about Shakespeare's procedures which have yet to be addressed. Shakespeare's way with character can be observed fully only in the business of constructing an entire play, and of arousing and developing an audience's interest in its action. None of the characters is independent: all are made progressively clear by interaction with one another. This has already been observed when considering how Aumerle and the Earl of Salisbury draw King Richard to reveal more of his thoughts and to learn about himself, and so help an audience to understand his deep rooted instability. Portia and Bassanio in *The Merchant of Venice* may be said to test each other, even while they are conscious of no such motivation. A process which challenges the resources of a character, and then unlocks or half-reveals what has been happening under the words of the dialogue, is constantly at work in the progress of a play, so that we may say that Shakespeare's characters are conceived for such inter-play and are progressively defined by it.

During performance a sense of gradual discovery is so strong that it is tempting to believe that a trick has been worked, that the author has revealed a finished concept one step at a time, creating puzzlement only to give us the pleasure of later clarifi-cation. But so many and various are the 'interpretations' which have been found for his characters, and what audiences have experienced is often so delicate and personal, that it is much more likely that Shakespeare was himself engaged in a search and that his mind was always reaching out as he wrote. The play texts offer a joint enterprise in which author, performers, and audi-ence are all adventurers in a changing world which the words set in motion, on stage and in co-operative minds.

Shakespeare seems to have been attracted to certain characters in the books he read because he wanted to live through them and explore the nature of their beings. Sometimes he used people he met in real life in the same way, and those he had seen on stage in other people's plays or had invented for his own pleasure. But he did not take possession of these persons as he found them, accepting and assuming their characters as if he were an imper-sonator taking on a number of clearly defined roles. His charac-ters may have been derived from numerous sources, but then they drew on his imagination, and when set in action on the stage they are offered life on their own terms with the co-operation of everyone concerned with the performance. They provided means for Shakespeare to reach out towards untold possibilities of being, and for others to continue the process afterwards.

Shakespeare's relationship to his characters was free and gen-erous, and he was bold enough to follow them into an amazing range and depth of experience. He worked on the boundaries of his own consciousness, so that he left scarcely any sign of taking words or actions for granted by resorting to habit, cliché, or single-minded perception. His characters draw nourishment and new definition from everything that happens in the course of the play. Shakespeare imagined his characters in interplay, and he started a game which was meant to be shared among all the players.

The plays must therefore be understood dynamically, not in terms of fixed statements. We must watch for what can happen to the characters, looking beneath appearances and listening for what words obscure as well as what they seem to say. We must observe how positions change, how words are heard and *not* heard, how interplay between persons is an essential part of their beings.

*   *   *

Again *Richard the Second* offers scenes for this enquiry which are not complicated with imitation of the business of actual life or with subsidiary plots. A six-line sentence begins the play. In questioning John of Gaunt, Richard finds means to accentuate both his uncle's age and his honour, and yet to place him in a dependent relationship by indicating that he understands the limitations within which he will reply. With a strength of purpose which fills out each verse-line, the king lays down his measured question, but a short, amplifying phrase which ends the third line with two stressed syllables – 'thy bold son' – can give a further impression that much more is thought than is fully spoken: is this spoken in praise or blame, or as a test of Gaunt's attitude to Richard and to his son? A parenthesis just before the close of the speech establishes the king's own concerns – his 'leisure', over against more 'boist'rous' affairs of state. So tensions are half-concealed in this unfurling sentence and these can grow freely in the minds of listeners during the following silence, indicated by an incomplete verse-line following or preceding Gaunt's polite but very brief reply:

> *Enter* KING RICHARD, JOHN OF GAUNT, *with other* NOBLES AND ATTENDANTS.
> KING RICHARD   Old John of Gaunt, time-honoured Lancaster,
>   Hast thou, according to thy oath and band,
>   Brought hither Henry Hereford, thy bold son,
>   Here to make good the boist'rous late appeal,
>   Which then our leisure would not let us hear,
>   Against the Duke of Norfolk, Thomas Mowbray?
> GAUNT   I have, my liege.
> KING RICHARD   Tell me, moreover, hast thou sounded him . . .

Perhaps old Gaunt bows elaborately in submission to his young 'liege' in order to avoid too close a contact; in which case physical disability may speak for him more strongly than his formal words. Or, possibly, Gaunt stands still, making only the smallest movement, and so indicates, with careful and defiant economy, that he is saying as little as possible. The eyes of the old grandee and his young liege will meet in challenge; in some way the two must confront each other, before Richard can proceed. The King must then pretend (or actually believe) that Gaunt has said all that he had expected by way of reply. Who is the more cunning or more covert? Does either yield an inch? Shakespeare has created a short confrontation which the actors can play with finesse or in fierce opposition. Meaning is not in words alone. Two highly motivated and opposing wills underlie them: Gaunt's son is risking his life, and Richard has been challenged in his right to rule as he thinks best. The words, which are elaborate and perhaps inadequate on the page, will be fortified on stage by the presence of the speakers and by their full consciousness of the situation. Interplay is so barbed that it can grab attention, even in the play's first moments, and can challenge understanding.

In *Forms of Talk* (Oxford, 1981), Erving Goffman has described speech as a series of movements in a game in which 'lead' is all-important and content depends on the context and manner in which the words are played. Such terminology is useful in trying to follow Shakespeare's engagement with his characters, but it falls short of his expertise, hardly coping with the interdependence of the speakers or the different levels of their consciousness. Moreover we must recognise that the dramatist is playing his own game with the characters and with their audience as well, all at the same time.

Shakespeare's scenes have the fascination of a cat's cradle. By releasing one strand or tightening another, their entire appearance changes. But that does not imply that the plays are merely a sequence of temporary revelations: each actor is engaged in continuous performance so that the changing impressions of each role will be held together by an unbroken thread located within that individual. The actors are uncommonly free to play as they choose or as proves possible, but their engagement throughout a whole play will lead them to make larger choices and exercise constraint on incidental decisions.

Shakespeare has marked no target at which an actor should take direct aim in a journey through the play, but he has provided holds and footings on which to base confidence and credibility. He has also created certain crises, shaped by especially powerful words or unambiguous action, when the actor's commitment to the moment draws on every possible resource and everything is at risk. The nature of a character, as it has been found during performance, is then laid on the line. Finally, when the play draws to its close, the audience is shown that the persons in the play have become whatever they have done; they cannot escape, but must do what by this time they have to do. At this point the text is often so simple that the words themselves would convey very little; sometimes they are ambiguous on the page. Either way the actor is required to endow the words with whatever sense of his character has been built up during the course of the play, as if the 'truth' were emerging on its own terms and in its own right. It seems as if Shakespeare has made provision for a final reckoning.

A play's last moments are the conclusion of a whole sequence of smaller but climactic and inescapable revelations. The first scene of *Richard the Second* continues with the two contestants having by far the most to say. Both reach stirring climaxes in which bloodshed and brute violence are opposed to loyalty and chivalric idealism, and the actors have to find their own balance within the confines of the text. The actor of Bolingbroke can heighten his denunciations with moral indignation as he accuses 'false Mowbray' of plotting the Duke of Gloucester's death:

> And consequently, like a traitor coward,
> Sluic'd out his innocent soul through streams of blood;
> Which blood, like sacrificing Abel's, cries
> Even from the tongueless caverns of the earth
> To me for justice and rough chastisement.
> (ll. 102–6)

Or Bolingbroke can remain entirely resolute, his streaming language controlled by cold ambition or nice political calculation. Or he can suffer, or seem to suffer, as a brother's murder echoes in his thoughts among tribal and pious instincts. But whatever way this speech is spoken, the actor must reach a climax at this point, because only one couplet remains to clinch whatever impression he has chosen. Then the king breaks a long silence to acknowledge – and so help to ensure – the overwhelming effect:

> And, by the glorious worth of my descent,
> This arm shall do it, or this life be spent.
> KING RICHARD　How high a pitch his resolution soars!

The king may have spoken ironically, seeking to deflate Bolingbroke's pretension, or he may have addressed Gaunt, Bolingbroke's father, to give a warning or reprimand; but no one says a word in reply and there may be a brief hiatus. Perhaps the king, noting this or ignoring it, covers up the effect of his single line and draws the action forward by turning to Mowbray: 'Thomas of Norfolk, what sayst thou to this?' Inevitably, at this switch of attention some clarification will be given, for how do the contestants face each other? How easily can Richard control the impassioned debate? What does the king think? But this moment is soon over, because it is not sustained by speech; it is a preparation for a later and more climactic revelation when the king draws the whole proceedings to an end. At this point there is no absolute need to betray signs of deep emotion and his voice need not hesitate.

In reply, Mowbray elicits from Richard an acknowledgement of Bolingbroke's closeness to the throne and then begins to answer the 'slander' to his own name. He establishes one kind of lead in this contest of truth by admitting to a crime against Gaunt, which Bolingbroke had not mentioned, and then lays down his challenge calmly, and with more show of respect towards the king than his opposite had used. Then the outcome is delayed temporarily by an almost comic interlude in which Richard calls upon Gaunt to help him heal the breach and both their intercessions are ignored. Once more Mowbray takes the lead, this time by a direct and more personal appeal to his 'dear, dear lord' – a tone which Bolingbroke has never attempted. This leads on to a conclusion in which a few very simple and large words are used repeatedly. He does nothing to implicate Richard in what he has done, but knocks hard on the doors of his master's memory:

> A jewel in a ten-times barr'd up chest
> Is a bold spirit in a loyal breast.
> Mine honour is my life; both grow in one;
> Take honour from me, and my life is done:
> Then, dear my liege, mine honour let me try;
> In that I live, and for that will I die.

> (ll. 180–5)

The force of these lines is unmistakable, but the actor is left to choose whether Mowbray is reckless or thoughtful, whether he seeks a special reward for his silence about the king's complicity in the murder of Gloucester, without actually asking for it, or whether he is falling back on the clichés of chivalry. In either case, Richard again delays judgement and directs attention to the opposite contestant. Is he afraid to answer Mowbray's plea?

As neither party agrees to give back the other's gages, with Bolingbroke the last to refuse the king's command, the conflict reaches a stand-off. Bolingbroke's words are solemn, and then he draws attention explicitly to his silent father, whose command, with the king's, he has refused:

> KING   Cousin, throw up your gage; do you begin.
> BOLINGBROKE   O, God defend my soul from such deep sin!
>   Shall I seem crest-fallen in my father's sight?

With a crude and savage image, he is soon attacking Mowbray again:

> . . . my teeth shall tear
> The slavish motive of recanting fear,
> And spit it bleeding in his high disgrace,
> Where shame doth harbour, even in Mowbray's face.
>   (ll. 186–95)

The result is remarkable and unexpected: in a single line, Richard silences both challengers: 'We were not born to sue, but to command!' The royal 'We', a calm yet rising rhythm, brevity, simplicity, and a reference back to a time before the present crisis: together these are irresistible. The actor of Richard has to rise to this climactic opportunity in some way: if his Richard is weak, he will shout; if strong, he may be cool and measured. Even if Richard hesitates or underplays the moment, its effectiveness is still assured, because no one answers. The play's action is dependent on how the line is spoken and how it is heard. Shakespeare has shaped the scene so that the audience is led to a moment of revelation in which inter-relationships are poised, held still for attention to be paid, and given force according to the involvement of each actor in the preceding exchange.

In his own time, the king continues with a subordinate phrase (which can have an ironic edge); and after simple assertions and commands he leaves the stage, no one daring to speak under this pressure:

> We were not born to sue, but to command! –
> Which since we cannot do to make you friends,
> Be ready, as your lives shall answer it.
> At Coventry, upon Saint Lambert's day.
> There shall your swords and lances arbitrate
> The swelling difference of your settled hate;
> Since we can not atone you, we shall see
> Justice design the victor's chivalry.
> Lord Marshal, command our officers-at-arms
> Be ready to direct these home alarms.

In one sense Richard is granting what both contestants have asked, but he does so on his own terms. The concluding couplet may hold another hint of irony, a mockery of the overblown pretension of these 'home alarms'; certainly it echoes the earlier 'command' and effectively demonstrates Richard's authority. After all the fiery and threatening words, Shakespeare has insisted that Richard take attention and in this interplay give an impressive revelation of his character which draws upon all that has happened so far. He leaves abruptly, holding his own counsel, and the others must follow in silence, in their own individual ways accepting his decision.

*   *   *

The vitality of Shakespeare's characters was achieved because he gave them independent life in his mind as he wrote. He seems to have put them all in charge of their own minds and beings, relinquishing command even while he remained responsible for every word they spoke. He then provided moments when they must show themselves with special clarity and force, while still explaining or defining very little.

If this seems an unlikely way to create intricate speeches and well-structured plays, other dramatists have recognised a similar process. Harold Pinter confessed to the *New York Times*:

> It may seem absurd, but I believe that I am speaking the truth when I say that I have suffered two kinds of pain through my

characters. I have witnessed *their* pain when I am in the act of distorting them, of falsifying them, and I have witnessed their contempt. I have suffered pain when I have been unable to get to the quick of them, when they wilfully elude me, when they withdraw into the shadows. And there's a third and rarer pain. That is when the right word, or the right act jolts them into their proper life. When that happens, the pain is worth having. When that happens, I am ready to take them into the nearest bar and buy drinks all around. And I hope they would forgive me my trespasses against them and do the same for me.[1]

Indeed an active imagination has led many other writers to say that they write in order to know what they think, or that their pen seems to have a power of its own or that they do not always recognise what they have written. In such a way Shakespeare gave his characters a life of their own.

Nothing could be further from the 'characters' which Shakespearian critics are fond of describing. These are constructs, delineated with several dominant drives, set in particular courses of behaviour, concerned with significant actions, provided with recognisable psychological features, and required to illustrate specific moral and political truths. We are sometimes told that his characters should be valued as representations of certain vices and virtues, and not as imitations of real persons in real life.[2] Such inscriptions would mean little to a strongly imaginative writer who could, lightly and seriously, hold many different beings together in his mind and provide words which help them towards an astonishing life upon a stage. Shakespeare seldom prescribed what should be achieved by his characters as they follow the course of the story; nor does it seem that he used them to prove anything by what they do and say – anything which could be stated clearly or, still less, defined ahead of performance. He may well have been surprised by the possibilities inherent in the words given them to speak. Like audiences at the Globe, who came again and again to a favourite play, he would not have been satisfied by any one performance which gave life to them.

On a few occasions, Shakespeare did introduce clear descriptions of one character by another, but these are limited views which are soon left behind or totally overturned. In *Twelfth Night*, Viola tells Olivia, 'I see you what you are: you are too proud'[3] and those words seem to sum up the Countess. But in their next encounter, it is Viola who is proud and Olivia completely at her mercy, probably on her knees:

> OLIVIA   ... by the roses of the spring,
>   By maidhood, honour, truth, and every thing,
>   I love thee so that, maugre all thy pride,
>   Nor wit nor reason can my passion hide.
>
>   (III.i.146ff)

In the same play Malvolio seems at first to live up to his name and little more: he is churlish and loves only himself. (Benvolio in *Romeo and Juliet* has another such name.) He is also said to be puritanical, but this is quickly counterstated by Maria, who sees him as a poseur: 'The devil a Puritan that he is, or anything constantly but a time-pleaser...'.[4] In the last scene he is shown in yet another guise: he clutches a piece of paper as if his whole life depended upon its evidence of another person's love and esteem. Finally, with 'I'll be reveng'd on the whole pack of you',[5] he is possessed by wholly other thoughts and feelings – hatred or, perhaps, fear of isolation.

Even when Shakespeare followed literary and theatrical conventions and created braggart soldiers who boast of their bravery and turn out to be cowards, that simple contrast does not sufficiently account for his characterisation. Don Armado, the braggart of *Love's Labour's Lost*, has a profound melancholy as well, and a courage in adversity; the simplicity of his love for a country girl can make him sound entirely credible when he tells the other lords that 'I have vow'd to Jaquenetta to hold the plough for her sweet love three year.'[6] The braggart Falstaff is proved a coward by Prince Hal and by the audience, several times over, but he is also a man of great resource and, on some occasions, remarkable courage: the Lord Chief Justice does not daunt him and Hal's rejection does not wholly deflate him: 'I will be as good as my word', he tells Justice Shallow, and rallies his friends by assuring them 'I shall be sent for soon at night.'[7] Pistol's very name proclaims him to be a 'swaggerer', but he is more than the 'fustian rascal' whom Doll Tearsheet scorns;[8] he can be generous and eloquent in interplay with Falstaff and, after the loss of wife and honour in *Henry V*, he defies both old age and Fortune by swearing to return to England and become a cut-purse. Pistol has a streak of glory and another of graft which may be uncovered and so light up the play: conventional first impressions prove unreliable.

At the end of *The Tragedy of Othello*, the hero seems to sum up his own life and complex character. He speaks

> Of one that lov'd not wisely, but too well;
> Of one not easily jealous, but, being wrought,
> Perplexed in the extreme; of one whose hand,
> Like the base Indian, threw a pearl away
> Richer than all his tribe; of one whose subdu'd eyes,
> Albeit unused to the melting mood,
> Drops tears as fast as the Arabian trees
> Their med'cinable gum. Set you down this:
> And say besides that in Aleppo once,
> Where a malignant and a turban'd Turk
> Beat a Venetian and traduc'd the state,
> I took by th' throat the circumcised dog,
> And smote him – thus.
>
> (V.ii.347–59)

But despite its assured tone, this speech does not tell everything; and this hero may not yet know all about himself. As Othello kills himself, Lodovico comments 'O bloody period!', marking only how the violent and cunning suicide contrasts with the dignified and temperate assessment of self-worth. But Gratiano goes further – 'All that is spoke is marr'd' – asserting that this last deed devalues other achievements and denies his own verbal estimation of himself. For the actor a vast range of possibilities opens up at this last moment, but in fact he will accomplish only what his performance up until this point, and at this moment, will allow him to do. He will have to summon physical strength for his suicide, and then he must change once more as he approaches Desdemona, whom he has just killed and whose dying word had been spoken in an attempt to save his life. (Othello had said that this was at the cost of her own soul.[9]) Speech is now simple, almost to the point of naivety:

> I kiss'd thee ere I kill'd thee. No way but this –
> Killing my self, to die upon a kiss.
>
> (ll. 361–2)

But *die* had subtle sexual meanings and 'No way' can refer to many different kinds of necessity. Besides, the effect of the words will depend a great deal on what actually happens. Is this intended kiss achieved, or does Othello fail to reach Desdemona? If he succeeds in reaching her and so dies close to her or embracing her, is he able to choose where he kisses her dead body? Then how does he kiss her: slowly or quickly, passionately, tenderly, sensuously, victoriously, or clumsily? Cassio's immediate assessment that Othello was 'great of heart' outdistances other assessments, including Othello's own, but it does not specify anything that is usually termed a 'characteristic'. Gentle, earnest, violent, or assured, accommodating all the accidental variations that are bound to occur in the staging of such actions, the actor will make a different final impression at each performance. The 'character' will have grown slowly and perhaps hesitantly during the interplay of all five Acts, and now the audience's sense of what Othello is will be finely tuned by the tension and quiet in which the last words and actions are played and the performance summed up.

*   *   *

In *All's Well that Ends Well*, a play with a greater than usual number of characters whose names seem to declare their natures, Shakespeare has an anonymous Lord meditate upon character:

> The web of our life is of a mingled yarn, good and ill together. Our virtues would be proud if our faults whipt them not; and our crimes would despair if they were not cherish'd by our virtues.   (IV.iii.67–70)

Such oppositions are too glib to account for the intricacies of interplay in Shakespeare's plays, but they do suggest that sense of conflict which is inseparable from the progressive unmasking of an inner 'truth' for their characters. Hamlet attacks those who would 'pluck the heart out of [his] mystery',[10] because that is not a simple matter; it is a complex and divided one. Later he says that

> . . . in my heart there was a kind of fighting
> That would not let me sleep.
>
> (V.ii.4–5)

Just before his last encounter with Claudius, he tells Horatio: 'thou wouldst not think how ill all's here about my heart; but it is no matter. . . . It is but foolery; but it is such a kind of gain-giving as would perhaps trouble a woman' (V.ii.203–8).

Engagement with Shakespeare's major characters involves conflict and confusion as well as progressive clarification. Edmund in *King Lear* speaks very early on of the 'fierce quality' of his being,[11] and most of his words and actions bear this out. But at the very close, as he pants 'for life', he comes to respect a very different peace-making instinct:

> Some good I mean to do,
> Despite of mine own nature. Quickly send –
> Be brief in it – to th'castle; for my writ
> Is on the life of Lear and on Cordelia.
> Nay, send in time.
>
> (V.iii.243–7)

This change of attitude is so surprising that no one is ready to act upon his instructions until he urges them a second time. Somewhere, within Edmund, has lain a contrary impulse, and an actor's task is to give this credibility 'despite' all expectations.

From time to time the interplay of performance forces characters to change tack and discover new resources which effect revolutionary purges within themselves. Their natures are wrenched to new purposes, and the innovation may so puzzle them that it seems like an enforced madness. Immediately before the duel at the end of the play, Hamlet sounds almost bemused at what he has done and what he has become:

> This presence knows,
> And you must needs have heard how I am punish'd
> With a sore distraction. What I have done
> That might your nature, honour, and exception,
> Roughly awake, I here proclaim was madness.
> Was't Hamlet wrong'd Laertes? Never Hamlet.
> If Hamlet from himself be ta'en away,
> And when he's not himself does wrong Laertes,
> Then Hamlet does it not, Hamlet denies it.
> Who does it, then? His madness. If't be so,
> Hamlet is of the faction that is wrong'd;
> His madness is poor Hamlet's enemy.
>
> (V.ii.220ff)

Shakespeare's understanding, when he was writing, was essentially practical, aware of lived experience, attuned to the sensations of being, pragmatic, and exploratory. The beings he imagined in action were most alive in interplay with others and with different aspects of their own selves. He endowed them with a consciousness of ideals and a capacity for decisive words and deeds, but their effective identities as they are established by the end of the action depends on *how* they have been acted and *how* they have interacted with other persons in the drama. This is the true journey of a play, which Shakespeare shared with his characters and discovered as he wrote and as he saw the actors' performances.

The very beings of his characters are subject to change: they become what they were not, and their world seems to change with them. Of course, the events of the story in which they are involved bring about obvious changes; one king dies and another reigns; wooing ends in marriage and discord in a feast; villains are unmasked and kinship recognised. But more affecting and more surprising than all this is what happens within the beings of the characters. Much depends on performance, on what the actors bring to their roles; Shakespeare has shaped what they do and fixed their encounters with words but the focus at the end of the plays is on the entire being as made present by each actor of a role, rather than on any state of mind represented wholly by words or by specific actions.

Between Shakespeare's words and the actors' performances, the audience is presented with an image of a world at risk and in search for some unassailable truth. In this sense, Shakespeare's writing was pragmatic and exploratory, and his art potentially subversive. Thinking, for him, was not isolated from practice: that is the essence of his theatrical originality.

*   *   *

At certain stages of his career, Shakespeare seems to have felt the need for an almost unfettered exploration of an individual character on his or her own account. In *Hamlet* four hundred and thirty-five consecutive lines in Act II, scene ii, give full scope to the leading role; it is by far the longest sustained episode in the tragedy. Nothing much happens of importance to the plot: Hamlet dismisses Polonius, greets and tests the loyalty of Rosencrantz and Guildenstern, welcomes the players, hears a speech from a play, dismisses everyone with instructions to perform before the king; and then, with 'Now I am alone' (l. 542), he starts to 'unpack [his] heart with words' (l. 581) until he almost has to force himself to remember his duty as revenger and the plans he has set in motion to 'catch the conscience of the king' (l. 601). It is a stark fact that the whole of this long sequence could be cut without confusing the play's narrative: Hamlet is seen with the players again before their performance, when *The Mousetrap* could have been arranged; and he has other opportunities to test Rosencrantz and Guildenstern. The scene's main purpose is not to forward the action but to establish Hamlet's character, with whatever emphases, certainties, and mysteries the actor chooses to provide. The energies of his mind are here made evident, the boundaries of his concerns, the strength and resilience of his feelings. He dominates the stage, as prince, courtier, friend, player, revenger, and philosopher, and as the son of a deceased father and an incestuous mother. He responds to politicians, students, and actors, and he is reminded of the ancient heroes and heroines of burning Troy; but, for this scene, Shakespeare does *not* provide him with Horatio, the friend of his choice with whom he feels secure. His mind has to be resourceful as well as free, leaping ahead of every stimulus: he is aware of a 'god kissing carrion', the 'prison' that is Denmark, the absolute 'beauty of the world' (ll. 180–1, 242 and 307). His speech sparks with humour and savagery; he takes time to note what others think and to react to his own thoughts. Throughout the scene, Shakespeare has kept his leading character free for active interplay and so satisfied the exploratory nature of his own creative mind.

Hamlet's obsessions with sexuality and death have not, however, been brought into full play at this point and Shakespeare has been preparing for more intensive exploration. Thoughts of dying are more fluent as they rise in the self-questioning of the 'To be, or not to be' soliloquy near the beginning of the next Act, but the presence of Ophelia is needed to unlock his sexuality in a second scene, where the matter of the play seems again to be forgotten in favour of interplay. Seeing her, Hamlet is torn by conflicting reactions. The ordering of verse is soon thrown aside and his speech becomes alternately like hammer-blows and like broad, sweeping torrents. As Hamlet faces the polite and careful girl (who had been to him, for 'everymore', his 'most dear lady'[12]), self-command snaps, and he may almost stutter in repetitions:

> OPHELIA   Good my lord,
>   How does your honour for this many a day?
> HAMLET   I humbly thank you; well, well, well.
>
>   (III.i.90–3)

The Quarto text has only one 'well', and the repetitions provided
by the Folio may be no more than an actor's elaboration of the
moment; but together with the conventionality of 'I humbly thank
you', the abruptness of a single 'well' to the person to whom he
had 'of late made many tenders of his affection'[13] could indicate,
as the repetitions also could do, a shocking refusal to communicate. When Ophelia tries to return his gifts and so makes a physical
contact between the two of them almost unavoidable, incomplete
verse-lines indicate silences that challenge comprehension and
heighten tension. Hamlet's few words lead abruptly to bare-faced
lies, or else to savage and harsh equivocations. Then, abruptly,
Hamlet questions both her honesty and her beauty:

> OPHELIA   My lord, I have remembrances of yours
>   That I have longed long to re-deliver.
>   I pray you now receive them.
> HAMLET   No, not I;
>   I never gave you aught.
> OPHELIA   My honour'd lord, you know right well you did,
>   And with them words of such sweet breath compos'd
>   As made the things more rich; their perfume lost,
>   Take these again; for to the noble mind
>   Rich gifts wax poor when givers prove unkind.
>   There, my lord.
> HAMLET   Ha, ha! Are you honest?
> OPHELIA   My lord?
> HAMLET   Are you fair?
> OPHELIA   What means your lordship?

Ophelia's incomprehension draws an evasive and taunting reply,
and then a bitter, general reflection which carries, in its long-
paced, deliberate prose, a half-hidden regret or a desperate resig-
nation. She says nothing more until he turns to her with a simple
acknowledgement that he had loved her at one time. Her answer
makes him try to deny what he has said, blaming his own instinctive falseness, and then to send her away, repressing any

reply with a stream of revulsion, guilt and suffering:

> HAMLET   That if you be honest and fair, your honesty should admit no discourse to your beauty.
>
> OPHELIA   Could beauty, my lord, have better commerce than with honesty?
>
> HAMLET   Ay, truly; for the power of beauty will sooner transform honesty from what it is to a bawd than the force of honesty can translate beauty into his likeness. This was sometime a paradox, but now the times gives it proof. I did love you once.
>
> OPHELIA   Indeed, my lord, you made me believe so.
>
> HAMLET   You should not have believ'd me; for virtue cannot so inoculate our old stock but we shall relish of it. I loved you not.
>
> OPHELIA   I was the more deceived.
>
> HAMLET   Get thee to a nunnery. Why wouldst thou be a breeder of sinners? I am myself indifferent honest, but yet I could accuse me of such things that it were better my mother had not borne me: I am very proud, revengeful, ambitious; with more offences at my beck than I have thoughts to put them in, imagination to give them shape, or time to act them in. What should such fellows as I do crawling between earth and heaven? We are arrant knaves, all; believe none of us. Go thy ways to a nunnery.

Nothing in the play has prepared the audience for this, or for the sharp, practical question which suddenly nails Ophelia down to a precise answer:

> HAMLET   Where's your father?
>
> OPHELIA   At home, my lord.

Either Ophelia has lied to defend herself or she has assumed, artlessly, that her father has gone to his own apartments (neither of the two texts tells us if Ophelia had heard that her father had intended to eavesdrop on what Hamlet would say to her). Hamlet senses something false and he draws still deeper on his consciousness. Her simple-seeming words are answered with cruel repression and blatant sexual mockery; for Hamlet, at this moment, Man is a fool and sexuality a monstrosity:

HAMLET   Let the doors be shut upon him, that he may play
the fool nowhere but in's own house. Farewell.

OPHELIA   O, help him, you sweet heavens!

HAMLET   If thou dost marry, I'll give thee this plague for thy
dowry: be thou as chaste as ice, as pure as snow, thou shalt
not escape calumny. Get thee to a nunnery, go, farewell. Or,
if thou wilt needs marry, marry a fool; for wise men know
well enough what monsters you make of them. To a nunnery, go; and quickly too. Farewell.

Pressure continues and Hamlet is driven on, gripped by thoughts
of pollution, deceit, and meaningless stupidity, by his own passion, horror, and sexuality, all quickened by an urgent insistence
against which Ophelia can say nothing. Perhaps her prayer that
'heavenly powers, restore him!' holds Hamlet back from leaving
the stage and brings out his further denunciations and the assertion of his own madness and strength of will.

This scene can be horrific in performance. Both Hamlet and
Ophelia cry out in pain; both may weep; they struggle to hold on
to what they had previously thought secure, and are left
floundering. In most productions a moment comes when they cling
to each other, overwhelmed by tenderness, or loss, or sense of
danger. Much depends on how the actors respond to each other
in performance, without premeditation. But Hamlet's deep involvement with Ophelia will always be marked unmistakably in the
repeated and emphatic dismissals: 'Get thee to a nunnery. . . . Go
thy ways to a nunnery. . . . Farewell. . . . Get thee to a nunnery,
go, farewell. . . . To a nunnery, go; and quickly too. Farewell. . . .
To a nunnery, go.' These words can very enormously in sound, force,
meaning, and emotion, from performer to performer, and from performance to performance. They are opportunities for searing pain
or for affectionate love, experienced beyond the reach of full consciousness. No moment, so far, has been so deeply personal; by the
verbal repetitions Shakespeare has insisted that the actor takes
full measure of it and finds what is for him the truest rendering.

*   *   *

When two characters are drawn and then held together throughout a sustained scene, Shakespeare can use the interplay between

them in words and actions to insist on revelations that are involuntary and to some extent unconscious.

In *Much Ado About Nothing*, the energy of Beatrice in reproof and her sharpness in mockery, coming so soon after she has confessed her love, combine to inflame Benedick so that he accepts her call to 'Kill Claudio',[14] having asserted, only a moment before, that he would not do so 'for the wide world'. He seems able to confront her scorn and her eyes alight with passion only by promising to challenge his friend. His words of acceptance have an abrupt decisiveness which give the impression that he is both thoroughly 'engaged' and also at a loss to know why he is doing what he is about to do. He has been overpowered, and led into territory which he hardly begins to understand. Her physical presence after her confession of love, and then her words and manner of speaking have all combined to achieve this.

Such an impression of full engagement is both physical and verbal. For a scene in which strong heterosexual attraction between two persons is an important element in their meeting, this might be thought impossible to achieve in Shakespeare's theatre, where female roles were all played by young male actors who could not directly or completely represent female bodies and sensibilities. But, on the contrary, it is arguable that such scenes would not be so effective in melding complex impressions if two persons fully capable of mutual sexual arousal were in each other's presence. Physical closeness combined with spoken words are able to animate the sexual imaginations of audiences in ways exactly and freely in accord with their own fantasies only if these are not limited by sexual arousal actually occurring on stage. To witness sexual pairing and to imagine it happening are two different activities, and in the theatre, for an audience, the latter can be much the more powerful experience. In masks and when speaking elaborate lyric verse, and viewed from great distances, the actors of ancient Greece were powerfully real in their audience's minds. In the present time, puppet plays and masked performances are known to provoke responses strongly charged with a sense of immediate sexual arousal. An audience can be convinced that the mask has changed, that it sweats with passion or weeps in frustration. What is necessary to set an audience's imagination to work is a clear physical element in performance, together with closely and intimately sensitive verbal interaction; and these Shakespeare provided for scenes of love and sexual arousal, as for all his plays' action.

In *Measure for Measure*, Isabella awakens Angelo's desire without realising that her appeal for a brother's life has brought her into dangerous intimacy, and has filled her words with sensuous images and pressing, uplifting rhythms. When Angelo takes her involuntary cue and has to hold back his desire, he finds himself doing so with words that still further suggest and arouse his own need to possess. When Isabella has left the stage, he acknowledges how he has become infected by the interplay against his will and judgement.

> ... it is I
> That, lying by the violet in the sun,
> Do as the carrion does, not as the flow'r,
> Corrupt with virtuous season. Can it be
> That modesty may more betray our sense
> Than woman's lightness?
>
> (II.ii.165–70)

When two characters know that they are equally attracted, as in *Antony and Cleopatra*, the interplay is less intense but wider in scope, and perhaps even more subtle and unconscious in effect. These two are free to 'sport' and 'wrangle',[15] and the next moment to move off stage elated by each other's presence. The action of Antony taking leave makes Cleopatra hesitate and draw back into her own thoughts, until she names the overwhelming power of her desire. Antony replies in a mixture of reproof and admiration, and so then she is drawn to acknowledge the pain inherent in her love and their involuntary conflict:

> ANTONY   I'll leave you, lady.
> CLEOPATRA   Courteous lord, one word.
>   Sir, you and I must part – but that's not it.
>   Sir, you and I have lov'd – but there's not it.
>   That you know well. Something it is I would –
>   O, my oblivion is a very Antony,
>   And I am all forgotten!
> ANTONY   But that your royalty
>   Holds idleness your subject, I should take you
>   For idleness itself.
> CLEOPATRA   'Tis sweating labour
>   To bear such idleness so near the heart
>   As Cleopatra this.
>
> (I.iii.86–95)

As they face each other, Cleopatra is aware of how he stands there and how she gazes upon him:

> But, sir, forgive me;
> Since my becomings kill me when they do not
> Eye well to you.
>
> (ll. 95–7)

Here interplay both establishes the moment, in all its deep feelings, and also indicates the longer engagement in which both try to manage their feelings by striving to understand them. Although Shakespeare knew that these scenes would be played by two male actors, he achieved such subtlety in his words and the physical performances they can inspire on stage that audiences accept the sexual reality of the relationships in their imaginations with a fulness which outstrips both words and physical action. When playing them, actors must follow the words, allowing intuition, physical response, sensation, intelligence, and feeling to draw them into the interplay. So they may communicate even when they do not fully achieve the inward nature of the characters they portray. They are instigating, through their performance, the same kind of progressive exploration which Shakespeare first undertook in his imagination as he wrote out their parts.

Dialogue of this kind is an achievement which distinguishes Shakespeare from many other dramatists. Whatever purpose he had in view as he started to write a play – and there must have been some intention that held all together, some rope on which to hold as he worked his way through the play – such a purpose was not the delineation of individual characters whose natures had been settled at the start. Shakespeare travelled free in company with the imaginary persons who were involved in the play's action, seeking truth to each moment as he brought them into touch with each other. In this way he was able to entertain them all and discover the means to let them live, as if truly and fully alive, in the different performances of many actors.

Shakespeare's texts also fuel the imaginations of audiences and readers. Their role is to follow what happens on stage with their own imaginations, converting that into whatever takes life in their individual minds.

6

Openness

Two boards and a passion are, proverbially, the essentials of theatre, but a practising dramatist knows that this is not true. The vital element of an audience has been omitted. In fact, the boards of a platform or stage are not an absolute requirement. Theatre can happen anywhere so long as persons acting in a play are watched by other persons. The two necessary ingredients are actors and audience: no performance is complete without spectators because their presence clearly separates a play world from the real world, and because their response influences all that is said and done in the play.

Dramatists are acutely aware of this, because they have been taught by experience. Anne Jellicoe recorded the effect of travelling with a production of her own play, *The Knack*, as it made its way to the Royal Court Theatre in London. The opening was in Cambridge, where young audiences 'greatly enjoyed themselves' and reactions were quick and lively. Here jokes were often seen just before their point had been reached, and so spectators had the happy illusion that they themselves were being witty. Sitting among these audiences, the author laughed at her own work as never before. The next week the production went to the West Country town of Bath, where 'thin and elderly' audiences were 'confused and outraged by the play; it was too quick and off-beat in style for them and they had no point of contact with the characters'. They also found the play to be obscene, and protesting letters appeared in the local press. Perhaps this should have been anticipated, but Anne Jellicoe was to discover it for herself:

> Sitting in the auditorium amongst that audience, I did not want to laugh. More than that, the play appeared obscene to me. I had had a number of arguments with the Lord Chamberlain [who was then Official Censor] over certain lines ... [but] when these lines were said in Bath, and other lines which he had

never questioned, it seemed to me that the Lord Chamberlain was right – they were obscene.... I had no wish to be the author of obscenity.

Then the play went to Cardiff, without its author. In that theatre, she was told, the bar receipts had never been higher, and she is still wondering what that meant. At last *The Knack* came to London, where notices were good, but not reassuring to the audience. When the author saw the play again she had to ask herself: 'How could I ever have thought this play obscene? It's so innocent, it's so young.'[1] The witty play and the obscene play had become naive and juvenile; it had changed before the author's own eyes as the audience contributed its part to the performance.

Yet many dramatists today resist thinking about an audience when they write, forswearing any thought of a play's reception. From the start of his career, Harold Pinter declared that he was only 'writing for himself':[2]

> I write to surprise myself – to paint myself into a corner and say, how are we going to work out of this? And then to let the material breathe, and say, 'Oh, it's doing this, it's doing this....'[3]

Such writing is a lonely activity, an uncertain struggle in which the dramatist is so engaged with the fictitious world he is creating that thoughts about the response of a real audience could only disturb concentration and damage the work in hand. Even Edward Bond – determined as he is to tackle social and moral problems in his plays – has said that he is 'not at all' aware of an audience when writing:

> if you're in a bicycle race you have to *assume* that you can ride a bike – if you're always thinking about how you're doing it you won't win.... I have written very committed plays,... but I couldn't work by asking, what's the audience going to think about this, or what must I tell the audience this week.[4]

Dramatists usually start to worry about audiences during previews. The presence of a paying audience pitches the actors' performances higher and reveals what has to be changed to ensure that everyone goes home well satisfied. While no production has ever been dragged from total disaster to success by this means, it has helped many find their most acceptable form or style. For new plays the period of adjustment is often crucial: lines can be cut from the text and others added; whole scenes may be re-written, eliminated, or hugely augmented; narrative can be simplified or complicated, motivations modified, keywords emphasised. The script, like everything else in the production, will be finely tuned with the help of its audience. Throughout previews of Peter Shaffer's *Amadeus* (1980) major changes were effected. At one time Salieri had appeared in a straitjacket, overpowered by madhouse officers, but all that disappeared before the official first night. Peter Hall, the director, had discovered that:

> it's important we do not present the story entirely through Salieri's eyes. There must be a tension between what the audience sees and what Salieri describes. A difficult balance to achieve.

The process of adjustment went on until the last possible moment: Paul Scofield, playing Salieri, had to beg author and director to stop giving him new lines to speak: 'they were, he said, like nails going into his head ... there was no time for more'.[5]

Shakespeare could not have identified with any of these writers. He had no opportunity for fine-tuning during a run of performances, in order to please an audience. For him the process of staging a play was very different: few company rehearsals, no previews, and no director to take charge. Above all, his audience did not sit in the dark waiting for a finished production to be presented to them. They were active participants all through a performance and as an actor himself Shakespeare had first-hand experience of this. Some of his characters speak of it: in *Julius Caesar*, Casca notes how the 'tag-rag people' clapped and hissed Caesar 'as he pleas'd and displeas'd them, as they use to do the players in the theatre'; in *Measure for Measure*, the Duke dislikes to 'stage' himself to the public and to submit to its 'loud applause and Aves vehement'; in *Henry the Eighth*, the Porter speaks of the 'youths that thunder at a playhouse and fight for bitten apples'.[6]

The sense of an audience close around the stage, in the same light as the actors, would have become instinctive to Shakespeare; no one on that stage could forget them, any more than a street-theatre actor today could begin to think about holding attention without being constantly aware of interplay with the spectators. Shakespeare continued to act at the Globe until the winter of 1603, by which time he had written more than half his plays and was engaged on *Measure for Measure* and *Othello*. When he no longer faced the public, he was still an 'actor-sharer' in the company and part owner of both theatres in which his plays were performed.

*   *   *

Among twentieth-century dramatists, some expressionist, epic, environmental, or community dramatists are perhaps closest to Shakespeare, for they may well have their audience in mind at all times. His plays, like theirs, were intended to provoke response, and indeed relied on it, but clear differences also existed. Shakespeare did not want the stage to become an instrument for propaganda or a platform for argument. He never called for placards to tell the audience what was about to happen in a scene. His actors did not have to buttonhole members of an audience, nor did he place them all around a theatre, in the manner of expressionist plays of the 1930s or Peter Brook's production of *Oedipus* for the National Theatre in London in 1968. Besides, strict censorship, enforced by imprisonment and a ban on performances, did not allow the representation of current affairs of state or religion, or the use of political slogans and agitation.

Shakespeare never forced his hand with his audiences, but rather sought an open relationship. Each play offered a two-way engagement: the text's dramatic effectiveness could respond to the audience's involvement, and at times the audience would be told more than the characters in the play and so were encouraged to take their own initiative in interpreting events.

For some plays Shakespeare provided a Chorus, Prologue or Epilogue to address the audience directly. While these persons do not speak for their author, they are the closest indication we have of the kind of audience–stage relationship Shakespeare wished to encourage. Nearly all are gentle, free, and open in their approach. In *Henry the Fifth*, the Chorus accompanies the course of the whole play and makes a special appeal for collaboration, as well as the more usual requests for forbearance, patience, attention, or applause:

> Piece out our imperfections with your thoughts . . .
> (I.Prol.23)

> Follow, follow!
> Grapple your minds to sternage of this navy . . .
> Still be kind,
> And eke out our performance with your mind.
> (III.Prol.17–35)

> Yet sit and see,
> Minding true things by what their mock'ries be.
> (IV.Prol.52–3)

Shakespeare knew that an audience could make or break a play. In *A Midsummer Night's Dream*, Duke Theseus protests that even from 'tongue-tied simplicity' he knows how to 'pick' what pleases himself and so enjoy good 'sport'.[7] Later on Shakespeare has made the same critic defend inexperienced actors by arguing that

> The best in this kind are but shadows; and the worst are no worse, if imagination amend them. . . . If we imagine no worse of them than they of themselves, they may pass for excellent men. (V.i.210–14)

In the same vein *Henry the Fifth*'s Chorus requests:

> And let us, ciphers to this great accompt,
> On your imaginary forces work.
> (I.Prol.17–18)

Between the 'ciphers' or 'shadows' on stage and the audience surrounding them in the theatre, a mutual trust should develop.

In Prologues and Epilogues, Shakespeare had his actors promise 'to strive to please you every day', 'to conjure you', 'to please you, day exceeding day'.[8] Begging for applause, they offer their 'toil' and their 'amends':

> Ours be your patience then, and yours our parts;
> Your gentle hands lend us, and take our hearts.
> (*All's Well*, Epilogue)

Only once, in *Troilus and Cressida*, is there a major change of tone:

> Like or find fault; do as your pleasures are;
> Now good or bad, 'tis but the chance of war.
> (Prologue, 30–1)

But this Chorus disclaims the confidence 'of author's pen or actor's voice', and is dressed in armour as befits the 'argument' of this play.

Shakespeare worked for a connivance between actors and audience, and came to depend on that response from them. So his plays would take wing; the actors could take risks and join in the hunt, and the audience would be free to imagine strange wonders. When all goes well and a play by Shakespeare moves from rehearsal to performance, a meeting occurs: the actors 'play' the audience, captivate it, ride and control it; they both indulge and release the audience, so that it also rises to the occasion. The game is mutual, a shared celebration, an adventure in interplay; and so every performance is unique. On both sides, imagination can be awakened as if for the first time, by means of all the activity which has been energised by Shakespeare's words. The texts were created in expectation of such an event, which would always be, in some measure, unprecedented.

*   *   *

Massed spectacle and loud sounds are an effective way of capturing an audience's attention. (They always have been, long before modern technology had so hugely increased their power.) Shakespeare knew this and would sometimes use a stage full of actors and have them processing, running, crying, shouting, praying, singing, waiting. On occasion he would add stage-machinery, fireworks, loud noise, drums and trumpets, flags, insignia and weapons of various sorts. But these means leave little to the imagination of an audience, which has nothing to do but submit to the show of force. Shakespeare would more often take the opposite route, paring everything away until all that the audience saw was a single actor standing alone on an empty stage. That performer, talking in front of an audience in the theatre, gave Shakespeare direct access to the audience's understanding and imagination. The play's impact was not confined by this narrow focus, because what happened on stage was less powerful than what happened inside the heads of the audience as they responded to a performance: there the drama would be fully realised. Through one person's performance, led by the words set down to be spoken, Shakespeare invited his audience to listen and to watch, and also to react: to hear and see behind the words and the actor, around, beneath, and through them, and to imagine much that was beyond them. Soliloquies allowed Shakespeare to conjure a whole world into existence in the minds of his audience; they provided times of great openness, when both actor and audience were free to explore and create.

Soliloquy was a common stage device in Elizabethan days. Translations and imitations of Senecan tragedy had given currency to the conventions of ancient tragedy, with straight-talking protagonists and informative messengers. The comedies of Plautus were yet more widely known, with slaves and gods speaking their minds in full confidence; characters entering a scene would tell the audience where they came from and what they thought was happening – and sometimes they asked what they should do about it all. Medieval mystery cycles, dramatising the Bible story, used soliloquies so that God could make his purpose plain, prophets and angels foretell the future, and erring men and women explain, plead, offer praise, and question. In all these plays soliloquies lay ready for Shakespeare to use, and he did so from beginning to end of his career in ways which developed the free interplay they offered between stage and auditorium.

Shakespeare's early plays rely on the lone actor's infectious energy: syntax, metre, rhetoric, rhythm, imagery, all affect the audience without conflicting interest or contrary focus of attention. More than that, the soliloquies invite interplay with the audience by using the same devices which were used to bring the play's characters into interplay with each other. So, in *Titus Andronicus*, after a crowded and eventful opening scene, Aaron the Moor is left alone and his soliloquy starts by playing on the present moment:

> Now climbeth Tamora Olympus' top,
> Safe out of Fortune's shot, and sits aloft . . .

But soon he stops in his tracks, and there is a silence. Two words, 'So Tamora', with the rest of the verse-line left blank, provide a hiatus, a vacuum which the audience's thoughts will variously fill. Perhaps Aaron plays for attention, by adding some physical reaction to enforce thoughts he does not want to put into words. He then goes on to speak of *how* Tamora has triumphed, and what he, himself, will do:

> As when the golden sun salutes the morn,
> And, having gilt the ocean with his beams,
> Gallops the zodiac in his glistering coach
> And overlooks the highest-peering hills,
> So Tamora.
> Upon her wit doth earthly honour wait,
> And virtue stoops and trembles at her frown.
> Then, Aaron, arm thy heart and fit thy thoughts
> To mount aloft with thy imperial mistress,
> And mount her pitch . . .

To enjoy such a soliloquy, the audience has to follow the speaker's thoughts and in their own imaginations find the means to understand the silence and the switches of attention. The audience travels forwards as Aaron does, even though his sentiments may be shocking or his full meaning hidden. As Aaron, the actor can now pose a question, directly to the audience or to himself, and know that no pause is needed because the spectators are already with him in their imaginations:

> Away with slavish weeds and servile thoughts!
> I will be bright and shine in pearl and gold,
> To wait upon this new-made emperess.
> 'To wait,' said I? To wanton with this queen,
> This goddess, this Semiramis, this nymph,
> This siren that will charm Rome's Saturnine,
> And see his shipwreck and his commonweal's.
> Hullo! what storm is this?
>
> (II.i.1ff)

The progression of imagery which follows his question and a sense of arrival, consequence, and alertness, take hold of the audience's attention, this time by leaping ahead and leaving them eager to catch up. As the empress's sons enter talking together, the audience will wait with Aaron for the best time to follow fresh game.

Shakespeare used soliloquies in so open a way that it matters

comparatively little whether the character addresses the audience
or speaks only for his or her own purposes. They are so written
that they draw the audience in and require its active participation if they are to be understood: the hesitations, questions, shifts
of attention, signs of self-awareness and self-evasion (both humor-
ous and affective), the amazing imagery, the sudden alertness,
all work to this end. In *Richard the Third*, as the Duke of Gloucester cheats and murders his way to the crown, soliloquies draw
the audience to share his thoughts, his wit ruling and teasing
theirs, just as in interplay it dominates the characters of the play.
Before the ill-omened final battle, his soliloquy, spoken as in a
dream, demands to be acted with physical immediacy and ner-
vous tension, because its words can only half-represent what is
happening in his mind and body. The audience will now find
itself working under pressure to keep in touch:

> Give me another horse. Bind up my wounds.
> Have mercy, Jesu! Soft! I did but dream.
> O coward conscience, how dost thou afflict me!
> The lights burn blue. It is now dead midnight,
> Cold fearful drops stand on my trembling flesh.
> What do I fear? Myself? There's none else by.
> Richard loves Richard; that is, I am I.
> Is there a murderer here? No – yes, I am.
> Then fly. What, from myself?

Here abrupt changes of mood and intention have to be activated,
if they are to be plausible and credible. The audience must sense
that Richard is driven, almost out of control, and then be ready
to feel that he needs some other person's pity. Yet at this point,
both actor and audience can go different ways, free to imagine
whatever their perceptions support. Is Richard concerned at last
for his own 'soul', or does he crave for 'love'? Words are very
simple and phrases short, and their effectiveness depends on what
they awaken in the minds of both actor and audience:

> I shall despair. There is no creature loves me;
> And if I die no soul will pity me.
> And wherefore should they . . .?

> > (V.iii.177ff)

The moment is over quickly, for Ratcliff enters unheralded and to him Richard speaks of his fear and the terror of his dream. Then he summons Ratcliff to go with him to 'play the eavesdropper' around the tents ('under' is Richard's word), to find out whether any of his followers mean to 'shrink' from him before battle. The immediacy of the soliloquy and its evident suffering have combined to set the audience's imaginations racing to keep up with Richard, but now it may be ahead in imagination, aware, as Richard is not, that his spirit has so shrunk that he is willing to act as a spy on his own troops. The audience watches the end of the scene as from another plane of being; that is part of the dynamics of interplay between audience and play.

As Shakespeare wrote he seems to have been constantly aware of the audience's potential for interplay, and used soliloquies as the most positive way to set this going, and to direct it. Aaron, Richard the Third, the Bastard in *King John*, Falstaff, Berowne, Bottom, Benedick, Viola, Romeo, Juliet – all these characters and more are established in the audience's mind by means of soliloquies which invite the audience into the workings of their minds by an act of its own imagination. An interplay is set up which seems to put the audience in possession, so that later it will follow these characters at times when they speak no words at all: when Romeo and Juliet are dead on stage and other characters try to sort out their responsibilities; when Benedick, confronted with Beatrice, is speechless or stupefied; when Falstaff is on his knees before the new king and has to listen in silence; when Viola has only heroic words to answer Orsino's frustrated rage and none at all as she goes off stage with him at the conclusion of the comedy. Shakespeare came to trust his ability to arouse the audience's imaginations, so that it was in their minds that his plays became fully alive.

*   *   *

Shakespeare was not only creative in himself, but the cause of creativity in others. Soliloquies were only one in a wide range of devices which he used to ensure the free and imaginative engagement of an audience.

The first scene of *Hamlet* begins with an interchange between soldiers and Horatio, in which all are straining to see and then to understand the Ghost,[9] so that by the second scene, when the prince is one member 'among others' at the court of King Claudius and his mother, the audience is prepared to search out the 'young Hamlet'. At first, however, it hears only bitter, tantalising wordplay from him:

> KING   But now, my cousin Hamlet, and my son –
> HAMLET   A little more than kin, and less than kind.
> KING   How is it that the clouds still hang on you?
> HAMLET   Not so, my lord; I am too much in the sun.
>
> (I.ii.64–7)

Perhaps Hamlet's first line is spoken aside, to himself or to the audience, but it could be spoken without restraint to the king his uncle. In any of these ways, it would baffle full understanding of what Hamlet is trying to say or do, and break the previous interchange between characters. Here Shakespeare seems to challenge the audience to guess or to imagine what is that 'within which passes show' (l. 85). Then comes the soliloquy with which Hamlet is more fully presented and, in its harsh transitions, repetitions, progressive imagery, questioning – 'Must I remember?' – and in its sudden stoppages, which are like seizures, his very being seems to lie open to the audience's apprehension. The soliloquy stops finally, when Hamlet addresses his 'heart' and not the audience: he may have heard Horatio and others entering or, perhaps, he is so aware of his own helplessness that he allows his thoughts to go no further:

> It is not, nor it cannot come to good.
> But break, my heart, for I must hold my tongue.
>
> (ll. 158–9)

By any reckoning Hamlet is one of the most complex of Shakespeare's characters, and a series of soliloquies is only one of the means which encourage the audience to enter imaginatively into his very personal and frightening predicament. The play's narrative is handled so that a prolonged two-way chase is sustained between him and the king, during which the audience knows more than either one of them and so thinks ahead and anticipates events. In interplay with Rosencrantz, Guildenstern and Polonius, and perhaps with Claudius, Gertrude and Ophelia, Hamlet has asides to draw attention to what dialogue cannot express. At the performance of *The Mousetrap*, the play with which Hamlet hopes to 'catch the conscience of the king',[10] his outspoken gibes while sitting with Ophelia ensure that the audience is alerted to watch Hamlet as much as either the play or the king. Yet here it cannot be in full possession of what he thinks; its imagination must either fasten on what can be held in the mind from among his savage, jocular wordplay or, failing to understand his words, sense only that some unspoken need or unprecedented pain is now at work. By this time in the play, a complex web of interactions is pulling the audience's attention in many ways, testing and widening its imaginative involvement.

When Hamlet returns after his journey to England, in Act V of the play, he has no more soliloquies of any length. In apparently casual manner, his thoughts are drawn out by the Gravedigger (who had started to dig graves the day Hamlet was born), by Laertes mourning Ophelia's corpse, and by the king. But on the other hand, his mother seems only to silence him. Now Shakespeare appears to be placing obstacles in the way of the audience's understanding of Hamlet's deepest, self-driven consciousness. Perhaps he speaks for himself, as if in soliloquy, as he is about to leave the stage near the close of the first of the two scenes:

> Let Hercules himself do what he may,
> The cat will mew, and dog will have his day.
>
> (ll. 285–6)

This couplet will taunt anyone seeking full understanding; the king cannot respond, beyond 'I pray thee, good Horatio, wait upon him', and the audience is placed in much the same position, however much it craves to know more.

At the start of the last scene, Hamlet seems to be offering a full and open account of himself to Horatio. But his friend's lame responses together with the pressure of events which is made apparent in Hamlet's own exclamations, needless repetitions and emphasis, imagery, and occasional withdrawals from explanation, continue to awaken the audience's sense that all is not yet capable of immediate comprehension. Then Osric and 'a Lord' (who was cut from the manuscript that lay behind the Folio text) draw out other responses. Hamlet's readiness to spar with Osric using his own weapons of conceited speech may amaze the audience, as it does Horatio, even as laughter tends to take over. When Osric has gone, Hamlet's explanatory speech is equally baffling, voicing a concern with the 'state of Denmark'[11] that has not been heard so clearly since he was called to witness the ghost. Perhaps this speech was confused in Shakespeare's manuscript and later scripts, for it seems to have puzzled the compositors of both good texts, so that neither makes fully acceptable sense:

> 'A did comply, sir, with his dug before 'a suck'd it. Thus has he, and many more of the same bevy, that I know the drossy age dotes on, only got the tune of the time and outward habit of encounter – a kind of yesty collection, which carries them through and through the most fann'd and winnowed opinions; and do but blow them to their trial, the bubbles are out.   (V.ii.181–8)

Somewhere here, among repetitions and strange imagery of dugs and dross, the audience may be able to feed its own ideas of the prince, the time, an outward habit of encounter, the oncoming trial. In turn, the Lord also awakens a strange response, because Hamlet then goes on to say that mankind lives and dies according to some providence that has thought for a sparrow, and that 'the end' – his end – will come almost of its own accord. Very simple words echo the Bible's trust in a beneficent and all-powerful God, a thought entirely new to Hamlet and one that seems to reduce his role to one of merely passive submission. The hero enters his final 'trial' (see ll. 181–8 quoted above) still prompting the audience to remain open to new impressions.

A set speech about his 'madness' to Laertes and the assembled company, interchanges about the fencing foils (not knowing Laertes' treachery, as the audience does), the shortest of addresses to his mother, some taunting of his opponent – 'I pray you pass with your best violence' (l. 290) – the 'incensed'[12] fighting, followed by a threefold killing of the king, with two poisons and a rapier's point, all draw the audience's attention strongly forward towards each succeeding event. There is little doubt of the play's effect on its audience here: all is caught up with *what* happens, rather that with *how* it is happening. Indeed the final deaths succeed each other so swiftly that the exact means of some of them may remain obscure to watchers in the theatre. Then comes a much slower passage, with the off-stage sound of Fortinbras's approach and Hamlet struggling to speak. Yet even now Shakespeare arranged, very specifically, that Hamlet should not 'tell all', as once he had said an actor should:[13]

You that look pale and tremble at this chance,
That are but mutes or audience to this act,
Had I but time, as this fell sergeant Death
Is strict in his arrest, O, I could tell you –
But let it be.

(ll. 326–30)

The last words that Hamlet is given are the puzzling 'The rest is silence' (l. 350): the audience must rely on its own imaginations to sense whether this is spoken in despair or satisfaction. Does he want to say more and cannot, or does he long for the 'quietus'[14] that is death? Do these words express a sudden horror as he faces death? The actor will guide the audience in one direction or another, but the context of this speech ensures and enhances the verbal ambiguity. Does Hamlet have to struggle to get his words out? (The Folio text adds a still more meaningless 'O, o, o, o.' before he dies.) To whom are his last words addressed? They could be, like a soliloquy, spoken for himself or to the theatre audience; they could be spoken to those assembled on stage, explaining that he is unable to say more; or to his friend Horatio, in an attempt to console him. The ambiguous words may continue to disturb the audience while Horatio follows them, in a quite different vein, with pious consolation and a prayer that angels should sing Hamlet to a comfortable 'rest'. Then the audience is given yet another prompt to make its own responses when Fortinbras orders military honours for a prince who has not been 'put on' to a fair trial.[15]

*   *   *

Playing upon an audience's understanding and imagination was so fundamental to Shakespeare's sense of dramatic action that a *tendency* to soliloquise is present in all the plays. Extended soliloquies and asides to be spoken away from the stage were only special cases of an openness to the audience which grew naturally out of a mode of dialogue which encouraged openness and interplay between characters. Looking back on *Richard the Second*, [16] we can mark a surprising number of sentences or shorter phrases as incipient soliloquies. Early in the first scene, for example, as Richard continues to address Gaunt, a couplet will stand out in the dialogue:

> High-stomach'd are they both and full of ire,
> In rage, deaf as the sea, hasty as fire.
>
> (ll. 18–19)

Perhaps this should not be directed to Gaunt, since he could scarcely accept this condemnation of his son without remonstration. If the words are spoken as a soliloquy, they are able to suggest that sense of doom and self-torture which will later surface strongly from within Richard's consciousness: not clearly or consciously here, but like a fault-line which may be sighted fleetingly by some among the audience. When Bolingbroke speaks a little later, he is already six lines into his speech of condemnation when he says explicitly that he turns to address his accuser; so he may have started by addressing his wider audience on stage and off. On the other hand, Mowbray's 'The blood is hot that must be cool'd for this' (l. 51) seems to be addressed to no one but himself, or to an audience other than the contending Bolingbroke.

In the scene of Richard's return from Ireland,[17] the king's tendency to soliloquise nearly takes over from dialogue altogether, although he is never actually alone. He tends to move outwards from whoever confronts him on stage, towards the audience in the theatre, and to play upon its imagination for a sympathy that can transcend the present moment and its concerns.

Such openness seems to have been instinctive to Shakespeare and it was certainly suitable for the open form of the theatre itself at that time, with the audience on three sides of its main acting-area and in the same light as the actors. To leave these spectators entirely to their own thoughts as the characters press forward in absolute concentration on what is happening on stage would be fine when the action is itself exciting – a chase, duel, battle, crucial argument, or murder can always hold attention – but when the characters are only preparing for such bold encounters or trying to respond to their outcome, there would be the opportunity, and perhaps the need, to draw the audience into imaginative engagement with them and encourage its independent participation. Shakespeare's creative mind must have thrived on this openness, because he experimented continually with its instigation, development, and manipulation. His plays hold everyone spell-bound when this interplay is freely enjoyed.

*   *   *

When Shakespeare came to write *King Lear*, some ten years after *Richard the Second*, from the start of the play he used formal soliloquies and strongly marked asides to draw the audience to think with and for numerous characters: Edmund, Kent, Gloucester, Edgar, and the Fool all have soliloquies when they are on stage by themselves; Cordelia has numerous asides. But Lear himself is not at first so open to the audience; he is never alone until, on the heath in the storm, he sends the other characters off stage. It seems as if Shakespeare had decided to resist the audience's desire to enter into the mind of Lear. He provoked its interest in him, of course – the king's actions are often unexpected, and are widely and variously discussed – but he kept the audience at a distance, allowing only momentary openness in angry outbursts, stunned repetitions and hesitations, and silences of incredulity or helplessness, all of which begin to seem like oncoming madness. Perhaps Lear is most clearly revealed in the early Acts in the surges and basic energies of his speech, which seem increasingly unsatisfied, like the cries of a great animal physically restrained against its will. The Fool's comments speak directly to the audience about Lear, but treating him as a butt for ridicule rather than giving information or providing entrance to the processes of Lear's mind. At last, having exclaimed against the storm in all its power, and fearing 'madness', Lear refuses to take cover:

> KENT   Good my lord, enter here.
> LEAR   Prithee go in thyself; seek thine own ease.
>   This tempest will not give me leave to ponder
>   On things would hurt me more. But I'll go in.
>   In, boy; go first.

This last is to the Fool, who in a moment more will leave so that Lear is left alone to 'ponder' on his pain. Perhaps Kent remains to watch over him, but if so Lear does not know this. At first, even now, he does not speak to the audience or to himself; nor does he pray as he said he would. Rather he addresses unnamed 'wretches', who are without all help:

> You houseless poverty –
> Nay, get thee in. I'll pray, and then I'll sleep.   (*Exit* FOOL.)
> Poor naked wretches, whereso'er you are,
> That bide the pelting of this pitiless storm,
> How shall your houseless heads and unfed sides,
> Your loop'd and window'd raggedness, defend you
> From seasons such as these? O, I have ta'en
> Too little care of this! Take physic, Pomp;
> Expose thyself to feel what wretches feel,
> That thou mayst shake the superflux to them,
> And show the heavens more just.
>
> (III.iv.22–36)

At the centre of this speech is one single and separate sentence
that speaks undoubtedly for Lear himself, and seems to be addressed to no one else: 'O, I have ta'en Too little care of this!'
Then immediately he addresses 'Pomp', the attribute of the power
by which he has lived until this moment. The sentiment he now
expresses, although conventional, is like nothing he has said before: 'Expose thyself to feel what wretches feel'; and coming after
an admission of guilt that seems to be wrung from within, it has
an amazing impression of being true to Lear's deepest instincts.
It is the moment when the audience can at last respond directly
to Lear, according to how each member thinks and feels. Words
alone do not indicate the power of this speech: in the strategy of
the play as a whole, this is where Lear's openness to the audience in soliloquy becomes an indispensable element of the drama.

For Lear, moments of true soliloquy are all very short, and in
the last scene they interweave with simple and urgent dialogue,
so that the audience comes closer than ever before to the hero of
this tragedy as he speaks of loss and love, of anger and disbelief.
It is neither a simple nor an obviously strong conclusion, and it
is capable of arousing many different reactions. To those on stage:

> He knows not what he says and vain is it
> That we present us to him.
>
> (V.iii.293–4)

Shakespeare provides no message for the audience, but rather, a
scene into which spectators enter, even against their will. Talking
to his few loyal friends and to Cordelia dead in his arms, Lear

struggles to share what hope he can imagine, and that purpose sometimes overcomes his anger and incomprehension:

> And my poor fool is hang'd! No, no, no life.
> Why should a dog, a horse, a rat have life,
> And thou no breath at all? Thou'lt come no more,
> Never, never, never, never, never.
> Pray you undo this button. Thank you, sir.
> Do you see this? Look on her. Look, her lips.
> Look there, look there!
>
> (ll. 305–11)

Again Lear's words are not particularly remarkable as individual words and they give contrary messages. The incontestable power of the scene in performance derives from Shakespeare's use of them to open up to the audience's imaginative understanding the conflicts within Lear, his suffering, determination, affection, anger, and even his domineering instincts. In company with all the assembled characters, the audience's imaginative collusion gives life to this scene, shares in the tragedy and in the act of finding whatever measure of understanding each one of them can reach.

* * *

Dramatists do not often speak about such effects. Perhaps they are achieved too rarely or too uncertainly. But actors will know from experience when they have worked or not. Constantin Stanislavski, having gone to see the great Italian actor Ernesto Rossi in *King Lear* in order to discover something of the secret of his success, recorded that at his greatest, at the end of the tragedy, Rossi appeared to do nothing:

> Unnoticeably, quietly, consequentially, step by step, Rossi led us up the spiritual ladder to the very strongest point of the rôle, but there he did not give us the last elemental burst of a mighty temperament which creates a miracle in the hearts and souls of men, but, as if he were being merciful to himself as an actor, often passed into simple pathos or used a bit of hokum, knowing that we would not notice it, for we would finish ourselves what he began and the impetus would carry us to the

heights alone, and without him. This method is used by the majority of great actors, but not all of them are so successful as Rossi was in using it.[18]

In the theatre there is surprisingly little discussion of effects like these, but sometimes they are self-evidently present. When audiences experience the powerful and refined grief of characters portrayed by Japanese Bunraku puppets, they are not affected by any very noticeable alteration of the puppet; they are responding imaginatively to what they see, prompted by the attendant music and narration, and by the discreet and watchful involvement of the three half-visible puppeteers. The audience can charge the small puppet with deep emotion.

Non-dramatic writers speak more readily about the kind of attention they seek from their readers. Near the beginning of *The Life and Opinions of Tristram Shandy, Gentleman*, Laurence Sterne has his hero explain:

> Writing, when properly managed – as you may be sure I think mine is – is but a different name for conversation. As no one who knows what he is about in good company would venture to talk all; so no author who understands the just boundaries of decorum and good breeding would presume to think all. The truest respect which you can pay to the reader's understanding is to halve this matter amicably, and leave him something to imagine, in his turn, as well as yourself.
>
> For my own part, I am eternally paying him compliments of this kind, and do all that lies in my power to keep his imagination as busy as my own.   (vol. II, ch. xi)

Theatre's 'conversation' has three participants: author, actor and audience, and is not so easily disentangled.

To appreciate the openness of Shakespeare's plays to the participation of an audience, they must be considered in entire performances, not only in separate moments and scenes. Glenda Jackson, speaking of rehearsing and playing Cleopatra, in Peter Brook's production of 1981–2, explained how performers can learn over many weeks just how an audience will respond, and how their judgement of the text changes in consequence:

... the middle of our second half – which is from Actium virtually up till Antony's death – I find ... very difficult. Although she's on stage all the time, she has very little to say and do. So the process of filling that out was at first a sort of murky area for me.... But the beginning of the last act ... is simpler because it's actually written in. The first time we did it on stage I felt that the play was much too long and that we were living on borrowed time as far as the last act was concerned. But since we played it in, it's been the most gripping part of the evening. It's an amazing act if you've got that flow going beforehand – the audience are quite happy to sit there for another 20 minutes and see how she does it. It's very, very potent when it works.[19]

As with Rossi and the Bunraku puppets, it is an audience which makes this play work; and the actor rides on its participation, leading it forward and controlling it. Having been held back from a knowledge of Cleopatra during the fourth Act, the audience will be the more ready to latch on to her very being when words mark out a territory for its entry and possession.

When actors and audience share in great deeds, strong emotions, and seemingly clear thought, theatre is at its most amazing and sustaining. For an experienced reader alert to this possibility something of the same kind can happen in the theatre of the mind, although the effect is usually slower and more reflective. Critics who ignore that all this happens, or pay no attention to it while they concentrate on minute details of textual meaning, will do an injustice to Shakespeare's skill as a dramatist and fail to account for some of the most distinctive qualities of his writing.

7

Happenings

In Elizabethan days, several lines of theatrical descent could be traced in the tragedies, comedies, and history plays to be seen on the London stages or studied in printed texts, but the degree to which Shakespeare's plays are related to any of these families can be traced only with great difficulty and uncertainly. In his own day, Shakespeare had Peter Quince in *A Midsummer Night's* and Polonius in *Hamlet* make a mockery of pedantic attempts to categorise dramatic genres;[1] and, when we try to consider the wider questions of his working methods and the structure and modes of the plays, the most notable feature of them all is an astonishing variety, both of inspiration and of finished product.

There is no such thing as a Shakespearian tragic form, no single method of structuring a comedy, history, or pastoral. Even the two or three parts of a history, in which a number of characters continue a single narrative line from play to play, differ in their handling of story and character. Clearly Shakespeare was not satisfied to repeat any pattern or principle of design, but for each play found a new engagement, a new disposition of the forces at his disposal. Perhaps this could hardly be otherwise if his dramatic structures were to be consistent with the wantonness of words in his mind or with his reliance on interplay between characters as a means of provoking and supporting lively performance.

*   *   *

For Shakespeare a new play probably began not with a form of drama, but with choice of narrative. Then, as he began to write, his characters would come alive in his mind and react to time and place, to events and to each other, becoming what they now are because of what he imagined them doing in the story he set out to tell, even though they would in turn modify that story as he was telling it. So the play began to take shape from its events and its characters.

In this, Shakespeare seems to have had the same taste as the majority of his audiences and readers. In the marketplace title-pages for plays would seek to attract purchasers by advertising what happened in the course of performance. In 1594 what is now known as *Henry the Sixth, Part Two* was recommended as:

> The First Part of the Contention betwixt the two famous Houses of York and Lancaster, with the death of the good Duke Humphrey: and the banishment and death of the Duke of Suffolk, and the tragical end of the proud Cardinal of Winchester, with the notable rebellion of Jack Cade: and the Duke of York's first claim unto the Crown.

Not content with calling *Richard the Third* a 'tragedy', the publisher proceeded to catalogue its contents and his own reactions to these happenings:

> The Tragedy of King Richard the Third.
> Containing, his treacherous plots against his brother Clarence: the pitiful murder of his innocent nephews: his tyranical usurpation: with the whole course of his detested life, and most deserved death.

Occasionally a bare title was allowed to speak for itself, but early quarto editions of *Henry the Fourth, Parts I* and *II, Henry the Fifth, The Merchant of Venice, The Merry Wives of Windsor* and *King Lear* were all given title-pages announcing the principal features of their stories. In 1609 *Troilus and Cressida* appeared at first with a plain title, but a second issue in the same year remedied that with a more persuasive sales-pitch:

> The famous History of Troilus and Cresseid, excellently expressing the beginning of their loves, with the conceited wooing of Pandarus, Prince of Licia.

Also in 1609, *Pericles* carried promise of a true and comprehensive relation of many events:

> The late and much admired play, called Pericles, Prince of Tyre,

with the true relation of the whole history, adventures, and
fortunes of the said prince; as also, the no less strange and
worthy accidents, in the birth and life of his daughter, Marina.
As it hath been divers and sundry times acted by His Majesty's Servants at the Globe on Bankside. By William Shakespeare.

For the public of that time, plays were recommended for incidents in their stories and the accomplishments of their actors,
more than for their literary pedigree.

In theatres, as in booksellers' shops, plays were known by their
stories. If we judge from surviving documents, efficient performance depended on a written schedule laying out how a play's
story was broken down into scenes, with lists of names showing
actors when they should enter onto the stage. This was known as
the play's 'plot' (or 'plat', as it was sometimes written) and it
was hung up in a convenient place back-stage to help the book-
keeper and tire-master organise proceedings, and to be consulted
as necessary by actors. On this master document, the play's division
into Acts was not important, but the unfolding of the story was
clearly marked as a sequence of scenes. The word 'plot' had several
other meanings. It was also the plan, outline, or 'skeleton' for any
literary work. George Puttenham used it in this way in his *Art of
English Poesie* (1589): 'Our maker or poet is ... first to devise his
plot or subject, then to fashion his poem' (III.xv). Some dramatists
set out their own 'plot' as the first step in playwriting. So Philip
Henslowe recorded in his day-book (or *Diary* as it is now called):

> Lent unto Benjamin Jonson, the 3 of December, 1597, upon a
> book [of] which he showed the plot unto the company, which
> he promised to deliver unto the company at Christmas next
> the sum of .... xx shillings.[2]

In *Antonio and Mellida* (*c.* 1599), as the stage fills with courtiers
priming themselves, John Marston has Feliche exclaim:

> More fools, more rare fools! O, for time and place long enough
> and large enough to act these fools! Here might be made a rare
> scene of folly, if the plot could bear it.   (III.ii.117–19)

In his plays, Shakespeare used the word 'plot' for a plot of
ground or for a cunning trick or stratagem.[3] His usual word for

the necessary backbone to a play was 'story', referring to its narrative authority and unfolding interest, rather than to its practical organisation or, as Puttenham might say, its 'subject':

> Vouchsafe to those that have not read the *story*
> That I may prompt them . . .
> (Henry V, V. Prol.1–2)

> Thus far, with rough and all-unable pen,
> Our bending author hath pursu'd the *story*,
> In little room confining mighty men,
> Mangling by starts the full course of their glory.
> (Ibid., Epilogue, 1–4)

('Our bending author' suggests someone labouring among books and papers to adapt a narrative for the stage – a picture doubly appropriate, as will be seen, to Shakespeare's fine-tuning of narrative and plot.)

> . . . this maid
> Hight Philoten; and it is said
> For certain in our *story*, she
> Would ever with Marina be.
> (Pericles, IV, Chorus, 17–20)

> Think ye see
> The very persons of our noble *story*
> As they were living; think you see them great,
> And follow'd with the general throng and sweat
> Of thousand friends; then, in a moment, see
> How soon this mightiness meets misery.
> (Henry VIII, Prol., 25–30)

But *story* is, of course, a word intended for the audience's ear. As author Shakespeare must also have been concerned in detail with the practical requirements of plotting, arranging for mangled starts and full courses, confining characters within the space allowed, pursuing time in a convenient sequence of very different appearances. Only by careful forethought could the 'bending author' arrange the events of one of his stories by using some twenty-five actors and their assistants. On two occasions the plays themselves refer to this process as if it were a prime accomplishment for a dramatist: 'An excellent play, well digested in the scenes', says Hamlet (II.ii.432), and the Prologue to *Troilus and Cressida* speaks of 'what may be digested in a play' (l. 29).

Whatever his story, Shakespeare had to digest its events into a plot which would suit the requirements of the stage. His source would present him with numerous individual characters and still more attendants, followers, and other persons involved with them in its main events; then his task would be to sort them out and arrange the story so that the necessary scenes could be played by a company of actors, their hired men, boy-actors, doorkeepers, and others who might be summoned to the stage. This alone was a complicated task: *Julius Caesar* names thirty-three characters and adds at least as many unnamed senators, citizens, guards, attendants, soldiers, together with a poet and soothsayer; *Antony and Cleopatra* has thirty-two named characters and a similar number of supernumaries, including a clown and a soothsayer. In the early *Henry the Sixth, Part One*, there are twenty-eight named parts, but in addition a huge crowd of annonymous supporters, a Mayor of London, a lawyer, several gaolers, a master-gunner and his son, a French general and sergeant, a porter, an old shepherd, lords, warders, heralds, officers, soldiers, messengers, attendants (both French and English), and fiends. *Richard the Third* presents hardly less complications in plotting, with thirty-six named parts and assorted supporting roles. The Prologue to *Romeo and Juliet* alludes to the 'fearful passage' of its story as the 'traffic of our stage' (ll. 9, 12), and both these phrases seem apt for the many shifts of scene involved in its performance and for the various kinds of processions, dances, disguises, night-scenes, music, stage-properties, stage-business, costume-changes, fights, duels, alarms, and surprises that the story entails. Generally the comedies call for fewer individual characters (although *A Midsummer Night's Dream* has twenty-seven named parts), but the twists and interlockings of their multiple story-lines are often more complicated and more rapid than those of other plays. The staging of any of Shakespeare's plays called for expert planning and control in the writing, and then a whole company of actors and others with their wits about them to bring all the events on to the stage. Only by plotting of the highest finesse would the playwright be protected from charges of incompetence.

*　　*　　*

The stories that attracted Shakespeare were seldom unusual and, in their very broadest outline, differed little from each other. Tales of wooing were used for comedies and of killing for tragedies, both modes presenting struggles for power or realignment which involve disguises and the testing of the characters' inner resources. For history plays, the death and succession of kings provided the major events in a pursuit of conquest or reconciliation. All Shakespeare's stories give occasion for opposition and conflict, often between different generations, families, races or sexes, and also for moments of agreement or peace. Some characters in each are involved in journeys, from home to a foreign country or some other strange place, from the familiar to the unknown. In many stories, supernatural, magic, or highly improbable events influence what happens to the characters or modify how they react – this is equally true of comedies and tragedies, though less so of histories, except in so far as some characters see an all-powerful Providence guarding the welfare of England. By the end of a play, the survivors of these events find themselves acting or re-acting in ways which would have been unthinkable and unrealisable at the start. This was perhaps the most distinctive feature of the stories as Shakespeare told them, but reduced to their general features their outlines were almost commonplace among the playwrights of the time. It is not here that Shakespeare's originality is to be found.

Only occasionally did Shakespeare choose an unusual story or invent one of his own. Quite frequently he took a suggestion from some play seen recently on the London stage. *The Merchant of Venice* followed two years after a revival of Marlowe's *Jew of Malta*, and there is record of a *Troilus and Cressida* four years before Shakespeare's; both a *Cleopatra* and an *Antony* had been written a dozen or more years before his *Antony and Cleopatra*. *Two Italian Gentlemen* was in print about seven years before the first performance of *The Two Gentlemen of Verona*. *King John*, *The Taming of the Shrew* and *Henry the Fifth* are each related to plays with very similar titles which were performed at more or less the same time. *The Comedy of Errors*, *Romeo and Juliet* and *King Lear* were based in part on plays already in print. Other pastoral comedies with enchantments of various kinds preceded *A Midsummer Night's Dream* and *As You Like It*. Even when Shakespeare did not work from any known source, notably for *Love's Labour's Lost, A Midsummer Night's Dream* and *The Tempest*, their stories were derived in a more general way from earlier plays by John Lyly (1554–1606), as well as being indebted to well-known folk celebrations and court entertainments. Perhaps one reason why Shakespeare was accepted so readily by actors and audiences was that in choice of subject-matter he did not strive to be either unusual or demanding: almost all his originality was in his handling of the stories.

His practice was far more remarkable in its painstaking search for different versions of his stories and careful choice of subsidiary material. Even by standards of the present time, when dramatists receive special funds to research a 'project' for a play, the amount of work Shakespeare undertook is impressive: he read widely, took notes, copied, conflated, rearranged, elaborated. His contemporaries would have known little of this and were usually content to think that he wrote with great ease and fluency: it was Shakespeare who described himself as 'our bending author'. Today we know differently because modern scholarship has revealed a dramatist who researched with great persistence and was accustomed to making very subtle choices between variant versions of a source-story. If all the books he consulted for a single play were to be placed side by side they might well cover a very large table; they could scarcely be carried in one pair of hands. Some volumes, such as Holinshed's *Chronicles*, were measured in feet rather than inches; and smaller ones, newly bound by hand, could not be laid open easily like modern paperbacks. Probably his actual source materials were never gathered together at any one time; books were still very expensive and, even if one had sufficient money to buy them, had to be located by searching in numerous small shops. We should perhaps think of Shakespeare as possessing his basic sources, but seeking variants elsewhere, skimming or absorbing numerous volumes and making notes, and sometimes borrowing a volume to take home if chance allowed. What is not in question is the complexity of this operation for almost all of his plays.

However the work was done, Shakespeare was a natural and even an obsessed researcher. A recent editor of *Richard the Third* has warned his readers that 'Discussion of the sources of *Richard III* entails the consideration of delicately interlocked issues.'[4] Much of the story came from the *Chronicles* of Ralph Holinshed (1577,

1587) and of Edward Hall (1548), but Shakespeare also used several of the short poems in *A Mirror for Magistrates* (1559), Sir Thomas More's *History of King Richard the Third* (1557), and, probably, the anonymous *True Tragedy of Richard the Third*, which was not published until the very poor text of 1594, perhaps the year of the first performance of Shakespeare's play. Besides all this reading of history, Shakespeare turned to other sources for certain episodes which were not in the *Chronicles*, such as the wooing of Lady Anne, Clarence's dream, and the chorus of wronged queens. Details for these and other scenes were found in works by Marlowe, Spenser, Kyd, Lyly, Thomas Lodge, and George Whetstone, and in Golding's translation of Ovid and several of Seneca's plays also in translation.

By Shakespeare's standards, the reading in preparation for *Richard the Third* was not particularly extensive, but it exemplifies how thoroughly and thoughtfully he would rework primary material to create a plot which exactly suited his requirements. By this means, he turned a sensational story of political corruption, murder and cruelty into a play which keeps suffering almost entirely off-stage, representing it only by speeches, which are placed after or before the events to which they refer. Clarence is stabbed on stage, but very suddenly and his body is removed immediately. Even the killing of Richard occurs off-stage, after he has made his last exit crying out 'A horse! a horse! my kingdom for a horse!' (V.v.13).

The story has been so 'digested into scenes' that cruelty and suffering are both bypassed, and in their place guilt, expiation, desperation, and hope of retribution are emphasised in the elaborate laments and curses of the women and in the ghostly procession of Richard's victims delivering oracular and admonitory utterances (V.iii.118–77). 'Why should calamity be full of words?' (IV.iv.126), asks the Duchess of York, and the answer is that Shakespeare has plotted his story in that way: he arranged matters so that an audience is able to respond freely to the central character, its wits sharpened by what it sees and hears, not blunted by watching the suffering for which he is responsible. Moreover, by having his hero introduce the action in many scenes, often assuming a new character as if he were an actor, and by giving him opportunities to address the audience directly and, in the closing scene, to reveal a most immediate and searing sense of fear and amazement,[5] he has also ensured that Richard takes the lead in awakening the audience's imagination.

Richard the Second shows other ways in which Shakespeare manipulated a story by means of his plotting. Here he was working with at least six main sources, but none gave authority for his retelling of the story. In his version, events are drawn closer together, and sometimes their sequence is altered, in order to create a stronger sense of consequence as one action leads to another. To achieve this he was not afraid to contradict everything he had read. For example, Holinshed's *Chronicle* provides much of the detail of the assassination, telling how Richard killed four of his assailants (in the play it is two), but it also tells that when he came near Sir Piers of Exton who was standing on a chair:

> he was felled with a stroke of a poleaxe which Sir Piers gave him upon the head, and therewith rid him out of life, without giving him respite once to call to God for mercy of his past offences.

In his reworking of this episode, Shakespeare gave Richard all the time he needed to condemn Exton for killing him, and then to commit his own soul to God:

> That hand shall burn in never-quenching fire
> That staggers thus my person. Exton, thy fierce hand
> Hath with the King's blood stained the King's own land.
> Mount, mount, my soul! thy seat is up on high;
> Whilst my gross flesh sinks downward, here to die.
>
> (V.v.108–12)

As Shakespeare plotted the moment of death, his Richard makes a more sustained impression than Holinshed's. He reminds the audience of his concern for kingship and his native land, of the throne on which he had sat in judgement, of his more recent 'hammering out' of the nature of his own identity. An audience may also be led to think that Richard is acting a part yet again, or that he has at last found the true centre of his life. Finally the plotting does not bring the focus to bear on violence, but on Richard's last resources in facing assassination.

The play's final scene, in which Richard's coffin is brought before the new King Henry in London, is again derived from Shakespeare's main sources, but changed in detail and effect. Holinshed tells how the murdered body 'was embalmed and cered, and covered with lead, all save the face, to the intent that all men might see him'; his account emphasises that Henry's plan was to ensure that no one should start rumours that his rival was still alive. The corpse was put on view in St Paul's cathedral for three days but the king was present only at Westminster for the mass of requiem, on which occasion he was accompanied by the citizens of London. In the play, the uncovered face as a means of identification is not mentioned: rather, a 'coffin' is brought on stage before the new king, and no one speaks of seeing any part of the corpse within it. The king is not with citizens, but surrounded by his nobles; and not at a solemn mass, but in his own palace immediately after hearing news of the defeat of a conspiracy. Exton arrives unannounced with the coffin, and immediately addresses Henry:

> Great King, within this coffin I present
> Thy buried fear.
>
> (V.vi.30f)

He gets no thanks, but is told 'With Cain go wander thorough shades of night' (l. 43). The king then protests his 'woe' to the assembled nobles and promises a voyage 'to the Holy Land, To wash this blood off from my guilty hand'. The nobles say nothing throughout the whole incident, although Henry addresses them directly. All these changes mean that the scene has been so plotted that, both on stage and in the audience, everyone will watch Henry closely for signs of a fear which cannot be buried, and of a will to rule. As the nobles follow their new king off stage, their movements and bearing will continue to express what these silent people feel but do not, or cannot, say. By all these changes Shakespeare has placed Henry's present motives under intense scrutiny and undermined any sense among the audience that the story has come to a full close with all issues resolved.

Richard the Second also shows that plot took precedence in Shakespeare's mind over any regular division into Acts and scenes. The five Acts into which modern editors have agreed to divide this text are of almost equal length except the fourth, and that is little more than half as long as any of the others. A clean and full break in the action, involving time and place, occurs only once, and then after the first scene of Act II and not between Acts.

Scene-length varies widely, from lows of twenty-four and eleven lines for Act II, scene iv and Act IV, scene iv, to as many as three hundred and thirty-four for Act IV, scene i, a scene which makes up an entire Act. Other Acts have variously four to six scenes each. Only a few of Shakespeare's plays are anywhere near regular in the balancing of Acts and scenes, but in these plays – *The Comedy of Errors* and *The Tempest* especially – regular proportions suit the handling of narrative. Usually Shakespeare was extremely free in these matters. *Love's Labour's Lost* has the second scene of Act V running to well over nine hundred lines, more than twice the number of any other. *Antony and Cleopatra* has so many short scenes in Acts III and IV, as one set of persons leaves to be replaced by another, that it used to be thought that Shakespeare had failed to master his narrative material; only in the twentieth century has the plotting of this play been vindicated in productions which recaptured an Elizabethan fluency in transition from place to place.

When Shakespeare had chosen his story, and its characters had begun to come alive in his imagination, the plotting of the action was his chief instrument for awakening and controlling the audience's attention; it was a dominant concern, more important than conforming to any preconceived division into five Acts or other regular shaping of the action. Indeed no moment in a play of Shakespeare's has been understood adequately until the plotting at that time has been taken into account, as well as the words that are spoken. To whom those words are directed and on what occasion, for what purpose, with what action, and with what response: nothing short of everything that happens on stage, moment by moment and in all its life-like yet contrived complexity, is the vehicle which provides the entertainment and carries the meanings of Shakespeare's plays. A reader should try to visualise all this, and a critic should try to analyse it: to quote what the characters say to each other is not sufficient basis for discussion of any issue in these dramas, even though many books of criticism and scholarship seem to assume as much. Every speech has its meaning or effectiveness according to the circumstances in which it is spoken, how it is instigated, how heard or not heard, and whether it satisfies or frustrates the expectations that Shakespeare has raised by the plotting of his story.

*   *   *

While conformist in choice of stories, Shakespeare's way of handling them was as much his own as his treatment of characters and dialogue. Three characteristics stand out, of which the most obvious is a tendency to complicate what happens on stage. While this is very evident in the comedies with multiple plots, like *A Midsummer Night's Dream* or *As You Like It*, all the plays show Shakespeare working in this way. In the histories, some characters who appear in only a few scenes are nevertheless developed as if for their own sakes: in *Henry the Fifth*, Pistol, Bardolph, Mrs Quickly (not least when off-stage), Fluellen, Bates, and the nameless Boy, and, among the French, the Dauphin and Herald, are all given independent attention in a number of scenes so that they each have a story which is told alongside those of King Henry and his nobles, and of the French King, Queen and Princess. Still more characters make an individual impact in single scenes.

In some plays 'supporting' characters are developed to such an extent that they pull attention away from the main narrative. In *Romeo and Juliet*, the Nurse and Mercutio are notorious examples of this and, towards the end, Friar Lawrence as well (in modern productions his speech of forty lines in the last scene is usually heavily or entirely cut). In *King John*, the Bastard often serves to draw strands of the political story together with almost no historical authority to do so, but he also takes the audience's attention on his own account and then he complicates rather than clarifies the political issues. Falstaff and Hotspur are developed so that their characters create independent centres of interest; they almost make the plays their own, not Henry the Fourth's or his son's.

Hamlet provides examples of complex plotting of almost every variety. Polonius engages Reynaldo to spy on Laertes, as Claudius uses Rosencrantz and Guildenstern to spy on Hamlet. Ambassadors go to England and return; Players arrive, rehearse, perform, and leave the stage in disorder, and a few of them return briefly. Ophelia and Laertes, as well as Hamlet, react to bereavement. Laertes gathers an army to confront Claudius; Fortinbras travels across Denmark with his own foreign army, and returns with it for the last moments of the play. Horatio, Rosencrantz and Guildenstern, Laertes, and Fortinbras are all very different and independent young men, and their ranks are joined in the last scene by 'young Osric', who owns 'much land, and fertile' (V.ii.189, 86); in different ways they all provide foils to Hamlet, giving fresh perspectives to the audience's view of him and of the court at Elsinore. There would have been more economical ways of bringing Hamlet back to Denmark in the last Act than by introducing two Clowns in a graveyard talking about their work.

Shakespeare made the story of Hamlet into such a long and complicated play that it can be cut to half its length and still make sense to an audience; for centuries it was never seen on the stage in anything like a full version. For example, when John Kemble played the prince at Covent Garden in the eighteenth century, the text of the last scene following the arrival of the King and Queen was cut by more than a quarter: this proved that there is no consequential need for Fortinbras or the Ambassadors to return to the stage (or to be in the play at all), or for Hamlet to exchange more than a few lines with Laertes before the duel, or for the future of Denmark to be considered, or for Horatio to speak of 'carnal, bloody, and unnatural acts'.

Modern texts, especially those which conflate the 'good' Quarto and the 1623 Folio, are seldom played in full. Differences between these two original texts probably represent Shakespeare's continuing interest in complicating the main story after his first version had been performed; for example, he was drawn to add something about the popular companies of boy-players, and to drop one of Hamlet's soliloquies which might have been thought to explain matters too simply (see II.ii.334–56 and IV.iv.32–66).

Sometimes complexity is most noticeable in the twists and turns which Shakespeare gave to the main story, when some more considerable action is to be expected. In *Much Ado About Nothing* a good hundred lines can be cut from Act V, scene i, without the audience noticing any loss: two old men's talk about grief and their attempt to fight a duel with two young men affect the main narrative hardly at all, but rather return to issues that have been presented before, with more complications. In *King John*, the emergence of the Bastard as spokesman for patriotism in Act V is almost to be expected, but by staging the niceties of Pandolph's diplomacy in Act V, scenes i and ii, and highlighting the personal struggles of Salisbury, Pembroke, and Count Melun throughout the same Act, Shakespeare has run the risk of confusing, if not frustrating, his audience, which wants to know at this point what is happening to John and his problems. Usually much of this text is cut for performance today, directors being impatient of that tendency to complicate which recommended itself to Shakespeare. Often it seems that he has written too much. Why should Gratiano arrive to fumble in opposition to Othello in the final scene? Why is the scene in England between Malcolm and Macduff couched in such an involved and lengthy manner? Why do the two surviving versions of *King Lear* vary the exposition towards the end of the play to such a degree that some whole scenes are easily expendable? The last scene of this play has been given so many twists of plot and changes of focus that no director today will accept every word of either text; very seldom, for example, are the bodies of Goneril and Regan brought back to the stage, or Edmund and Edgar allowed to account for all their experiences, or Albany allowed to remark on what he has forgotten. It would seem that Shakespeare wished to maintain several distinct perspectives and, to achieve this, was willing to lessen the build-up in effectiveness of the central action. In play after play, his plotting ensures that the leading character or characters do not take all attention; an audience eager to see a remarkable performance is kept waiting while multiple views of the play's action are given. A need to lessen the burden on the leading actors cannot entirely explain this because it often effects the opposite. Some restless quality in Shakespeare's mind had to find the means to prevent an audience believing that all has become clear and that a single response is all that matters.

* * *

As significant in Shakespeare's manner of plotting, but not so immediately apparent, is the introduction of an extended scene, usually about halfway through a play, in which a leading character is kept centre-stage not taking immediate action himself, but hearing reports of action elsewhere or criticisms of his own attitudes. The usual handling of a story will draw the main characters forward without resistance, sometimes impetuously so, as for Henry the Fifth before the battle of Agincourt:

> My brother Gloucester's voice? Ay;
> I know thy errand, I will go with thee;
> The day, my friends, and all things, stay for me.
>
> (IV.i.302–4)

Here the narrative line is taut, but just previously, before daybreak on what will soon be the field of battle, it had been quite as remarkably slack, the king being given all the time needed to react as he wishes to whomever he happens to encounter. Talking with Pistol, Fluellen, Gower, John Bates, Alexander Court, and Michael Williams, Henry hears and sees the effects of his own deeds as he leads these men towards battle and perhaps to their deaths. Immediately after this slow-moving episode, while there is still nothing that Henry has to do, Shakespeare has him fall to his knees in prayer and allows the audience to hear his deepest thoughts and feelings; for the first time he speaks of the guilt he felt for inheriting a throne which his father had won by insurrection and murder. His penitence, he knows, is 'nothing worth', despite 'contrite tears' and five hundred poor

> in yearly pay,
> Who twice a day their wither'd hands hold up
> Toward heaven, to pardon blood.
>
> (ll. 294–6)

Henry himself had alerted the audience to what might happen when 'the spirit is eased' and 'the mind is quick'ned':

> out of doubt
> The organs, though defunct and dead before,
> Break up their drowsy grave and newly move
> With casted slough and fresh legerity.
>
> (ll. 19–23)

But he did not know that he would find his own secrets revealed by this very process. Shakespeare has held the action back so that King Henry's quickened mind is set at ease and his very soul can show itself for what it is, speaking through an involuntary organ, like a ghost come to life.

In *Henry the Fourth, Part Two*, the dying king has a phrase which well describes this device in the plotting of a play: when Harry is 'moody', his brothers are told to

> give him line and scope
> Till that his passions, like a whale on ground,
> Confound themselves with working.
>
> (IV.iv.39–41)

When a play's narrative line is not pulled forward but notably relaxed, energies of thought and feeling can be expressed from within a character and the audience can be drawn forward not by following a plot, but by a growth in its understanding of the issues and the persons involved. Every play was given unhurried *entractes* of some kind. In *Richard the Second* as we have already noticed in Chapter 2, the scene of the king's return from Ireland takes the narrative forward only with the news brought by Salisbury and Scroop; it is an almost static scene in which Richard turns this way and that, alternately confident and in despair, and at one time holding the others back:

> For God's sake let us sit upon the ground
> And tell sad stories of the death of kings . . .
>
> (III.ii.155f)

At last he leaves precipitously, not daring to talk more. Much later, in another scene when alone in prison, Richard again has nothing to do but explore his 'still-breeding thoughts' (V.v.8), responding only to music played off-stage and the casual entry of a nameless groom who proves reluctant to leave and unable to say what is in his heart. The main narrative line has been slackened so that scope is given for Richard to disclose his state of mind and for the audience to be brought more in touch with the defeated king. The audience will be brought closer to the actor as well, for in this last isolation the whole part has to be given a convincing close; this is the moment in performance when the actor will tend to identify with his role most fully, because here Richard's very being is most deeply exposed.

In each play exploratory and revelatory scenes are used differently, and sometimes placed differently. In *Macbeth* the hero has demands for action placed on him right through until the last swordfight; even in the brief scene with the murderers (III.i.72–139), he seems driven to keep persuading the two anonymous men to murder when they have already pronounced themselves very ready to kill. In this play it is Lady Macduff with her boy, and Lady Macbeth when she is sleepwalking who are given time on stage when action is held back and they talk simply for the sake of talking or to prevent themselves from doing something else. In *Othello*, the hero is accompanied by Iago when otherwise he would have time and scope for free talk; and later he becomes too obsessed with action for this, until in the very last scene he takes centre-stage to speak for himself, and everyone else holds back from interrupting. In this play it is, again, the women who have been given 'idle' time: Desdemona among the waiting soldiers before Othello arrives in Cyprus, and Desdemona and Emilia as they wait for him to come to bed (II.i and IV.iii).

In *King Lear* a series of scenes on the Heath and then at the foot of Dover Cliff give the most extensive freedom from immediate action that Shakespeare ever devised; Lear is drawn into himself and, beyond all previous experience, finds his thoughts going out in sympathy to all 'naked wretches', to a seeming madman who is pursued by fiends, and to a blind old man whom he half-realises is Gloucester.

Freedom to react is not always unexpected and snatched from more pressing concerns. Sometimes a scene seems to have been introduced solely for the purpose of idle pleasure, as in *Twelfth Night* (II.iii.1–126) and the two parts of *Henry the Fourth* (*Part I*, III.i.192–262; and *Part II*, V.iii.1–81). In scenes like these, time seems to stand still and words are spoken from the heart which otherwise could not have been spoken. At ease in the Gloucestershire orchard, Falstaff welcomes the 'sweet of the night' and, when he exclaims to old Silence, 'Why, now you have done me right' (*2 Henry IV*, V.iii.71–2), the whole person of the fat knight may seem to be in those indulgent, unhurried words of good fellowship, even though laced with irony. In *Twelfth Night* during what Malvolio refers to as 'caterwauling', the call for a 'love song', without care 'for a good life', is sufficient to start some 'admirable fooling' in contrast with which other personal relationships in the comedy can appear both self-absorbed and fragile (II.iii.1–83).

The sheer variety of Hamlet's engagement in the long second scene of Act II establishes some of the furthest reaches of his thoughts and affections and shows how confidently Shakespeare would delay narrative interest. The prince enters aimlessly, reading a book, and for well over four hundred lines he does nothing except meet various persons whom he and the audience have met before. The plot of the play is forwarded at the very end of the scene when he plans to show the king a play, but until that point he is occupied only with taunting Polonius, testing his two friends Rosencrantz and Guildenstern, and welcoming the players, all to little practical purpose. The clear-sighted speed with which he moves among friends and enemies alike encourages an audience to share in the excitement with Hamlet and with the actor as he is discovering how best to give credibility to the glittering surface of the words and the changing consciousness behind them. The long scene opens Hamlet's being to an audience's gaze, a progressive disclosing of what Claudius will call 'something in his soul O'er which his melancholy sits on brood' and what he himself will later call the 'heart of my mystery' (III.i.164–5 and III.ii.356). Without this scene, Hamlet would not speak of the sun breeding maggots, of the hammering of 'words, words, words', of Denmark as a prison, of his bad dreams, of beggars, shadows, men, angels, a 'majestical roof fretted with golden fire', of dust, women, the tribute due to players, and much else; he would not have called for the horrifying speech about Pyrrhus or broken in on it with talk of a 'mobled queen'. Between audience and character, and character and actor, a collusion begins which will involve excitement, admiration, fear, and a passionate concern for some state of being beyond the reach of present knowledge.

In performance these episodes, which have been plotted by Shakespeare to be almost without a plot, cast such light upon the main characters that they receive from their audience a kind of acceptance which story-telling alone could not have achieved. Every play by Shakespeare is provided with some measure of this enlightenment and its effect continues long afterwards. For example, Desdemona's quiet and unhurried talk with Emilia immediately before their separate deaths, affects the audience's reception of the entire last Act of *Othello*. Falstaff's good fellowship in Shallow's orchard ensures that the audience feels the pain of Hal's rejection of him soon afterwards. After the second scene of Act II, the audience understands so much about Hamlet's contrary moods that he does not forfeit its attention during his violent treatment of Ophelia and Gertrude, his 'lugging the guts' of Polonius, or his frequent and apparently unmotivated delays. In reading a play-text, as in seeing it performed, sufficient line and scope should be allowed to the imagination for these scenes to reach their intended and reflective power.

Neither a description of a play's story-line nor a commentary on its principal and strongly-placed speeches will encompass Shakespeare's achievement; he was not only constructing a myth or seeking a single deed for a hero to accomplish. The plotting which holds back action and purposeful speech shows that the plays are also concerned with those workings of mind and body which usually remain secret.

* * *

Conclusions demonstrate a third characteristic of Shakespeare's plotting. The end of a story, whether that involves marriage, or victory in battle, or death, or some other decisive happening, always brings a final choice, a resolution one way or the other so that the audience feels free to leave the play and go home again. But Shakespeare, it seems, was never content for this to happen too easily, without the emergence of some additional, unexpected factor or some shift of focus giving a sense of surprise as well as satisfaction, as if nothing could be taken for granted. For the actors this means that right up until the very last moment they have to be alert to what is new and maintain some degree of improvisation, drawing still deeper on whatever they bring to their roles.

In the last two scenes of *Richard the Second*, a comparison with the sources of the play has shown how Shakespeare manipulated and altered what he had found to give Richard an eleventh hour change of spirit and to make Henry and his followers stand precariously in mutual suspicion. The *Chronicles* of Holinshed and Hall were written with clear notions of what lessons history could give, but Shakespeare's plays based on them do not work in that way. At the end of *Henry the Fourth, Part One*, Prince Hal is reconciled to his father, having saved his life in battle, but that is not all: Shakespeare also has him promise to corroborate Falstaff's entirely false claim to have killed Hotspur, the most dangerous of the rebels:

> Come, bring your luggage nobly on your back.
> For my part, if a lie may do thee grace,
> I'll gild it with the happiest terms I have.
>
> (V.iv. 155–7)

Falstaff hoisting the carcase on to his back is such a grotesque or pathetic figure that the actor of Hal needs to point these lines very carefully and judge, at the last moment, exactly what force and meaning he gives to them. In the concluding scene, which follows immediately, no one says how Hotspur was killed, but in the king's final speech, which points the action forward to *Part Two*, the audience may hear echoes of Hal's words to Falstaff which will reflect on what he says:

> And since this business so fair is done,
> Let us not leave till all our own be won.
> (IV.v.43–4)

Perhaps by this time Falstaff has arrived on stage having followed, as he said, 'for reward'; if so, the irony will be inescapable and Hal's commitment to the on-going action strongly questioned.

The end of *Henry the Fourth, Part Two* could scarcely be less like the expectations of anyone who had read the *Chronicles*. Prince Hal does succeed his father, but that occupies little of the last few scenes. From taking his ease in Gloucestershire, Falstaff has arrived in London; Doll Tearsheet is then carried off to prison, shouting curses on her persecutors; and Falstaff promises to deliver her. 'There roar'd the sea, and trumpet-clangor sounds!' exclaims Pistol in admiration (V.v.40), and at this very moment Henry enters for the first time as king, newly crowned and accompanied by all his train. He stops to confront Falstaff, and matters of realm which are the concern of a 'true history' have to wait until the very last lines of the play, when Prince John of Lancaster is alone on stage with the Chief Justice:

> PRINCE JOHN The King hath call'd his parliament, my lord.
> CHIEF JUSTICE He hath.
> PRINCE JOHN I will lay odds that, ere this year expire,
> We bear our civil swords and native fire
> As far as France. I heard a bird so sing,
> Whose music, to my thinking, pleas'd the King.
> Come, will you hence?   [*Exeunt.*]
> (ll. 104–10)

Here history is presented as in the *Chronicles*, but the audience hears of it as from a distance, from those who have to interpret sounds as quiet and joyful as birdsong. It will have heard a great deal more strongly the sounds of goodfellowship, fear, and ruthlessness in Henry's last speech to Falstaff – and much else besides, according to the way the play has run its wandering course and the actors have realised their parts in scenes invented and interpolated by Shakespeare.

In the last scene of *Hamlet* Shakespeare sprang his surprise with Fortinbras's entry claiming that he has 'some rights of memory in this kingdom' (v.ii.381). From the time when he appeared briefly with his army in Act IV until less than ten lines before this second entry, no one has even mentioned him. The audience knows nothing of the 'rights' he speaks of, and now he says nothing to substantiate them. Nevertheless it is Fortinbras who is in charge of the final moments, not Horatio, whose summing up of the story is rehearsed in very general terms. Quite unexpectedly, focus has been shifted away from the 'quarry' lying dead on stage, towards a future of which the audience is told very little.

Perhaps *Othello* has the most unexpected, unsettling, and incomplete conclusion of all the major plays. This is not brought about by introducing any new element, but by alterations to the story and the way in which the scene is plotted. For once, Shakespeare had derived the story from a single source in Giraldi Cinthio's *Hecatomithi*, available, so far as is known, only in the original Italian or a French translation. For the conclusion, however, he went his own way. Cinthio's Iago and Moor together pulled down a beam in the ceiling of Disdemona's bedroom so that her death might seem an accident; the Moor was then accused by Cassio and subsequently tortured and banished, to be assassinated later by kinsfolk of Disdemona. Iago lived on until he also was tortured for quite another crime, and so terribly that he was 'taken home where he died a miserable death'. The storyteller sums it all up: 'Thus did Heaven avenge the innocence of Disdemona.' In plotting this play, Shakespeare evolved a substantially new ending, as if his characters demanded a different judgement, and he also introduced uncertainty. His Iago is on stage to witness Othello's self-destruction, but by then his last speech has already been spoken:

> Demand me nothing. What you know, you know.
> From this time forth I never will speak word.
>   (V.ii.306–7)

This does not mean that he steps back out of focus so that the play reaches its conclusion without him. Quite the contrary: while he maintains silence, the other characters several times direct attention to him, Lodovico in the very last speech of the play ordering him to take responsibility:

> O Spartan dog,
> More fell than anguish, hunger, or the sea!
> Look on the tragic loading of this bed.
> This is thy work. – The object poisons sight;
> Let it be hid.
>
> (ll. 364–8)

Iago still says nothing, so that, when the bed's curtains are closed, only he of the three principals is left to make whatever impression on his audience each particular performance of the role achieves in this self-chosen silence. Shakespeare's plotting ensures that the audience scrutinises Iago closely and in some productions he makes the strongest impression, as well as the last, in this new ending of the story.

Some plays from their very inception must have been geared for an ending in which a number of stories would be offset against each other and the balance readjusted at the last moment. Comedies provide the prime examples. In the short penultimate scene of *As You Like it*, 'It was a lover and his lass', sung, riotously perhaps, by a couple of young boys, seems to set up an almost runaway lightness. Then, in the last scene, this is followed by Touchstone's more cumbersome entertainment of the company which is waiting for a conclusion: he asserts the weird, fulsome, and potentially dangerous world of honour with a sequence of imitations sorted into various verbal categories. This interlude will have life in performance only when the clown transforms laborious pedantry into a display of self-assurance, bringing laughter and pleasure to everyone on stage and in the theatre. Next comes the god Hymen, for whose very existence Shakespeare has done nothing at all to prepare the audience. His entry can make a wide range of effects, each capable of redirecting the course and mood of the comedy. It can provide a solemn, sensuous, and large-scale show, kept in check by the slow measure of its careful verse and music. But if the supernatural role of Hymen is played by an obviously unskilled mortal (Corin or William can be conscripted for the job), another range of effects is possible. Even the '*Still music*', required by a stage direction, may serve only to accentuate an overflow of ebullient good spirits, which can be supported by quick dialogue, neat rhymes and repetitions, and happy 'confusions' (see 1. 119).

Not content with all this volatile material, Shakespeare then brings on stage a third son of Sir Rowland de Boys, who is the second born and called Jaques, a very minor character in the story who seems to have been forgotten until this moment. He is used now to bring news that Duke Federick, marching with an army against his brother, has met an 'old religious man' whose talk has converted him from his purpose. Then, to make the conclusion veer course yet again, Shakespeare brings Jaques into centre-stage – the original Jaques, not the new and much younger one – and has him announce that he will go off to talk with the new convertite, for out of such persons 'There is much matter to be heard and learn'd' (l. 179). Before leaving he bestows his own idiosyncratic blessings to each pair of lovers, who are by now queueing up to begin a a final dance. For the senior and experienced actor who plays this lonely and wry satirist, this is an opportunity to make a mark at the end of his performance, the focus at least as much on him as on the joyful couples whom he addresses. Music and dancing follow, but when Rosalind steps out to address the audience, Shakespeare once more springs a surprise and causes yet further readjustment: against all convention, the young male actor emerges from under his stage persona of Rosalind to taunt the audience and 'conjure' for their applause, playing openly now with his own sexual attractions and desires.

In contrast with the comedies or histories, *Antony and Cleopatra* would seem by its very story to demand a single and settled focus as it ends with the queen's carefully prepared suicide within the safety of the royal 'monument', but this moment is disturbed by small and insistent details of plotting. Quite unusually the audience is shown Cleopatra dressing for the occasion, commanding with great dignity, 'Give me my robe, put on my crown, . . .' (l. 278). Yet two interjections, 'Yare, yare, good Iras; quick!' and 'So, have you done?' (ll. 281, 288), make clear that this operation takes considerable time and that any grandeur is offset by the queen's impatience. In a silent reading of the text, Cleopatra's final speech has measured calm and glowing lyricism, but when it is enacted both tone and tempo become uncertain because quick words and hurried movements will interrupt all the grandeur of thought and speech. As she kisses her servants farewell, a still greater surprise is introduced when Iras falls down suddenly, and dies without saying a word. The queen responds at once and regains the chief focus by implicating herself in her servant's death. However, she is then silent and, probably, quite still. Only after a pause, indicated by a half-line of verse, does Charmian offer an invocation, which associates this unexpectedly still moment with the darkening light which would actually occur during the latter part of a performance in the open-air Globe Theatre:

> Dissolve, thick cloud, and rain, that I may say
> The gods themselves do weep.

Now Cleopatra takes an asp to her breast, and as soon as she has felt its bite her words recall a baby sucking its nurse asleep. But the poison does not work quickly enough and she takes a second asp. Then, almost at once, she dies in the middle of a sentence, as if struck by an invisible and invincible blow:[6]

> As sweet as balm, as soft as air, as gentle –
> O Antony! Nay, I will take thee too:
> What should I stay . . .

Her end is not peaceful or dignified, as a description of Charmian's subsequent death makes plain: 'Tremblingly she stood,' it is said, 'And on the sudden dropp'd.' Cleopatra's death pangs after taking the same poison must shake her whole body in the same way. As she attempts to maintain her royal performance, dressed for the part and uttering glowing words, her struggle is so great that her crown is thrust 'awry' and afterwards Charmian will have to 'mend' it. When Caesar enters it seems to him that Cleopatra has died making a strong movement, striving to 'catch another Antony In her strong toil of grace' (ll. 316–17 and 344–5).

The audience is held in thrall not only by the words which are spoken, but also by the physical struggles involved in the suicide. In performance at the Globe Theatre, no one could foretell exactly what would happen because too much was prey to accident after the very minimal rehearsals with which the King's Men prepared for staging a play. The imaginary forces of the audience have to hold together both the grand image and the subterfuge by which it is created. When Caesar enters to wind up the narrative, his words give new impetus to the scene, but he has not witnessed what the audience has watched attentively and therefore he cannot respond so deeply and sensitively to Cleopatra's death. Inevitably he will be heard with some measure of disbelief or impatience. When the audience disperses after the play is finished, each member carries away his or her own image of a 'lass unparalleled', seen as if she had lived instinctively and cunningly before their eyes.

*   *   *

Sustaining or exciting narrative, strong stage images, clearly stated arguments or themes, powerful and special emotions: any of these Shakespeare could and did deliver, but the complexity of his imagination, evident in the way he plotted the scenes, insisted that any one effect was repeatedly offset by others. He created a great variety of opportunity and left the actors free to make their own choice and define each performance afresh as it develops on stage; and the audience is left free to find its own entry into what is happening.

This way of presenting a story for performance appears to be different from many in use today. While few experienced dramatists will have the plan of a play's action worked out ahead and then adhere strictly to it scene by scene during the writing, most do keep some idea or theme in mind from the beginning of their work, some image or characters they wish to create, an issue they want to tackle, a subject they intend to present. In *Timebends* (1987), his autobiography, Arthur Miller tells how he moved slowly from *All My Sons*, which opened in New York in 1947, to *Death of a Salesman* of 1949, and then started the longer journey to *A View from the Bridge* of 1955: settings, characters, phrases, and a subject gradually fixed themselves in his mind, and writing followed. Many dramatists could tell the same story, but with Shakespeare it would seem that the two processes ran concurrently, the play taking shape as he wrote, its distinguishing elements remaining 'in play' even after the writing was finished, up until the moment when actors took over the text and their performance defined an unrepeatable happening. To enjoy his plays or assess his achievement, a reader should try to respond to this inventiveness of plotting, which continues to unsettle expectations and free the imagination until the very end of a play's action. Every reading should suggest new meanings and discover new pleasure.

8
Meanings and Arguments

In our times Shakespeare's plays are always yielding up new meanings. Philosopher, psychoanalyst (Freudian or Jungian), theologian (Catholic or Protestant), sociologist, historian, Marxist, moralist, hedonist, sceptic, naturalist, poet and, by no means least, teacher, all reinterpret to suit themselves. Books are published about other books all proposing divergent meanings; an example is Harriet Hawkins, *The Devil's Party: Critical Counter-interpretations of Shakespearian Drama* (Oxford, 1985). Anthologists collect the newest of reinterpretations; an example is *Alternative Shakespeares* (London and New York, 1985) edited by John Drakakis, who notes in his introduction:

> Criticism is now an openly pluralist activity, with proponents of particular positions contesting vigorously the intellectual space which it has occupied. (p. 1)

Among Marxists, or Freudians, or feminists, there is no agreement, because each critic discovers new and different meanings in the very same texts, and even within a single scene or speech.[1] In Shakespeare's plays all readers find reflections of their own particular interests and so the various meanings that emerge are usually incompatible with each other. Few critics believe that any one interpretation of a play is the only possible one, but many will vigorously defend a reading they have proposed against others, as the most true, the most penetrating, or the most revealing.

Why should this be? Of course we live in a pluralist society and some people are paid to have views about Shakespeare and about what is called the critics' debate, in all its latest twists and confrontations. But the question remains why Shakespeare's plays should arouse such a very strong appetite for re-interpretation. It seems as if they were written in a way that positively encourages divergent opinions and embattled controversies, similar to the arguments which raged about the interpretation of a holy writ when the salvation of souls or defence of possessions was at stake. For Shakespeare's plays, the argument is not confined to the words of a text, the plays being re-interpreted with equal zeal in the theatre, where new 'concepts' are stamped all over the look and message of stage productions. Besides, ambitious actors continue a much longer tradition of finding new meanings in what they say and do, as they make the leading roles their own. No other writer in any medium has given rise to so much revisonist activity.

* * *

In some ways Shakespeare shared a positive delight in multiple meanings with other artists of his time. Traditions of biblical exegesis, whereby the persons and events of the Old Testament were interpreted as prefigurations of Christ's incarnation, death, and resurrection, encouraged an allegorical way of thought that became widespread and instinctive. Saying one thing was frequently recognised as implying something else, often something very different. According to St Thomas Aquinas, the scriptures contained twofold truths:

> One lies in the things meant by the words used – that is the literal sense; the other in the way things become figures of other things, and in this consists the spiritual sense.[2]

While biblical commentators believed that certain symbols had a divinely inspired multiplicity of meanings, it was natural that the mainstream of poets should follow their lead. Indeed, through several centuries, narrative poems and sonnets were designed so that they could be interpreted in more than one way. Topical, local, historical, mythical, religious and personal meanings cohabited in these works with descriptions of place, persons, and action. Epics, reveries, lyrical songs, and debates in verse and prose all were given double or treble meanings. All the arts were affected, so that paintings, sculptures, and even buildings and gardens, would be created so that they spoke with several voices, revealing hidden meanings to those who knew how to read them.

Multiple meanings were everywhere conspicuous in heraldic devices, hieroglyphs, and riddles, and Shakespeare's plays contain several examples of this taste for public puzzles contrived to engage and tease the mind of observer or reader. In *The Merchant of Venice*, mottoes, capable of various interpretations, are inscribed on the caskets whereby Portia is guaranteed to receive the correct husband, and in *Twelfth Night* the obscure and multiple meanings of the letter written by Maria in Olivia's hand are intended to perplex Malvolio. The witches' prophecies in Act I of *Macbeth* reveal all their secrets only at the end of the play. In *The Merchant* the lives of both Antonio and Shylock depend on a single phrase, which is given an entirely new meaning only after Portia and a lawyer are said to have 'turn'd over many books together' (IV.i.155). The very title of this play can be taken in several ways, for who is 'The Merchant' when more than one leading figure, besides Shylock and Antonio, ventures with money or inheritance, or buys and sells, or steals, or tries to do something of this kind, as if life were a matter of exchanging merchandise?

When he named his characters, Shakespeare would often change what he found in his sources to suggest several alternative meanings. Among the names he invented for *The Winter's Tale*, that of Paulina carries hints of the virtues of both Pallas and St Paul, Hermione those of Harmonia (a goddess of love) and Hermione (Helen's daughter), and also perhaps, in a punning way, of Hermes, messenger of the gods. The name Leontes refers unequivocally to the lion, but that creature could be reckoned both noble when compared with other beasts, and brutish when compared with mankind. Taking up hints like these, the action of the play can be interpreted in several ways simultaneously.[3] Stage properties had emblematic as well as practical meanings: flowers, fruit and herbs very obviously and specifically (for example, rosemary has meanings suitable for both weddings and funerals); swords (implying justice, as well as valour or sexual potency), books (implying pious, sceptical, or fantastic thoughts), rings (denoting love, devotion, and possession or bondage), jewels (for thoughts of wealth or sexuality). Articles of common use spoke for actions or aptitudes beyond their actual usage: staffs, tables, chairs, cushions, beds, brooms. In emblem books and portraiture, such multi-valent references were commonplace.

Censorship, which was considered a necessity of the times, also encouraged multiple readings and concealment. When poets wrote of Cynthia, they meant either the moon or Elizabeth the virgin queen, or more probably both. This much was commonplace and quickly recognised, and the censor stayed his hand. But when a writer wished to deal with actual current issues of 'state or religion' – twin subjects both absolutely forbidden on the stage – meaning had to be cloaked in personifications much less easy to interpret. It is generally agreed that some characters in *Love's Labour's Lost* allude to various persons involved in the rivalries of Elizabeth's court, but exactly who these people were and to what purpose they were evoked are questions still in debate. Queen Elizabeth believed that when Richard the Second appeared in a play on the public stage he was meant as an allusion to herself; and it could follow that Bolingbroke in Shakespeare's *Richard the Second* might be intended as a portrait of the Earl of Essex, the fatally active politician who was referred to admiringly in the Prologue to Act V of *Henry the Fifth*, but was very soon later to be executed for high treason. A writer in Shakespeare's day would often suggest two conflicting meanings, so that, when challenged by the censor, the more obvious and innocuous could be paraded as an alibi in the hope that the dangerous meaning would pass unregarded.

These habits belonged to many writers whose works do not give rise to the various and urgent controversies which have grown around Shakespeare's. The multiplicity of meanings found in his plays must therefore be due to his way of writing for stage performance rather than to the intellectual habits of the age, influential though those were. As we have seen, his characters were imagined as if they were independent living beings, present and aware in every faculty and sense, and interacting with other independently imagined characters. So what is said and done in a play is a reflection of lived experience as Shakespeare both knew and imagined it. The divergent opinions, prejudices, and passions encountered in his own life became inextricably woven into the texts of his plays and the very stuff of their action. For example, the exchange between Hotspur and Sir Richard Vernon examined in Chapter 2 (pp. 27–9, above) raises matters of state, inheritance, comradeship, psychology, social behaviour, religion, tradition, public relations, education. The intellectual engagement of these speeches concerns no less a subject than civilisation. No matter who is speaking, each character has been given his or her own standpoint and personal commitment, and since what is said on both sides of any argument is likely to be equally clear and convinced, each is as able as the other to catch a critic's attention. It is no accident that Shakespeare has become the source of quotations used by politicians and preachers of all persuasions, or that his phrases are now proverbs in use daily among many very different people.

Further scope for finding new meanings lies in the absence of any preordained idea of 'character'. The persons of these plays change, or at least develop, as the narrative draws them into different encounters; their experience deepens during the course of the action, and they seem to discover new meanings in the very act of speaking. Ideas change and loyalties shift, while ironies are found in the commonest of words. When King Henry concludes the first part of *Henry the Fourth* with the couplet

> And since this business so fair is done,
> Let us not leave till all our own be won.

the question of what is 'our own' is tantalisingly unclear. When his son, as Henry the Fifth, proclaims that it is death to say the victory of Agincourt belongs to anyone except God, the question of his motive for this becomes inescapable, and also of his meaning in the concluding lines of this scene:

> and to England then;
> Where ne'er from France arriv'd more happy men.
> (*Henry V*, IV.viii.123–4)

What does he mean by 'God' and who is truly a 'happy' man? Are the 'happy men' simply those who are satisfied, contented, and pleased, or are they just plain lucky? (All these were current senses of the word.) What did his father mean in the earlier play by 'fair' and 'all our own'? The way Shakespeare's characters speak of these and other essential matters is keyed to the speaker, the occasion, and, often, the listener: meanings collide with each other, or one will haunt another.

It is in the very nature of Shakespeare's plays that meanings multiply and choice between them is difficult. This is not to say that any one meaning is as valid as another; but rather that each will have limited value according to the context in which it arises and is identified. We find the meanings which suit ourselves, and the times and places in which we live. Other meanings arise in the theatre, given power by the actors' commitment to their entire roles and the physical context of the productions in which they appear. Each time Fortinbras concludes *Hamlet* the effect will be different:

> Let four captains
> Bear Hamlet like a soldier to the stage;
> For he was likely, had he been put on,
> To have prov'd most royal; . . .
> Go, bid the soldiers shoot.
>   (*Hamlet*, V.ii.387–95)

What a particular actor makes of Fortinbras as he speaks these words – a confident, callous, awestruck, or politically ingenious young man – and how another, as Hamlet, has ended his part in silence – confident, uncertain, hopeless, bitter, or courageous and unbroken in spirit – together with the management, tempo, and tone of the whole scene, will all effect whatever meaning arises, drawing some implications to the surface of the audience's consciousness and losing others.

One limitation, however, should be placed on the variety of meanings, one test applied to the worth of whatever we discover: all possible meanings, for readers or for audiences, should have a common dependence upon the entire action of the play, on all that happens on stage. Of course each stage performance will be different and in itself may suggest quite new interpretations, but certain events are enacted physically in all of them, and a meaning that is not well grounded in that substantial activity common to all performances can have only accidental importance, speaking more for the predilections and circumstances of the person who has discovered it than for anything intrinsic to the play as Shakespeare wrote it.

* * *

After the dumb show has indicated what will follow, in *The Murder of Gonzalo*, Shakespeare has Hamlet mock Ophelia's desire to know its 'meaning':

OPHELIA   What means this, my lord?
HAMLET   Marry, this is miching mallecho; it means mischief.

OPHELIA   Belike this show imports the argument of the play.

Enter PROLOGUE.

HAMLET   We shall know by this fellow: the players cannot keep
counsel; they'll tell all.

OPHELIA   Will a' tell us what this show meant?

HAMLET   Ay, or any show that you will show him. Be not you
asham'd to show, he'll not shame to tell you what it means.

(III.ii.133–42)

This dialogue does *not* tell us what kind of meaning Shakespeare
thought a play should have, or whether he thought it should have
one or many; but it does illustrate how his audiences might demand a clear and graspable interpretation. It also tells us that a
play was expected to have an 'argument' that could be abstracted
and communicated in advance of performance. A little later,
Claudius will ask:

KING   Have you heard the argument? Is there no offence in't?

HAMLET   No, no; they do but jest, poison in jest; no offence i'
th' world.

(ll. 227–30)

'Argument' is a word which recurs in Shakespeare's plays. When
Falstaff turns the conversation to rouse everyone's spirits, asking
'Shall we have a play extempore?', Hal replies, 'Content – and
the argument shall be thy running away' (*1 Henry IV*, II.iv.270–
2): he knows what the play will be about, what it will 'show'
everybody. The dying king in *Henry the Fourth, Part Two* judges
the effect of his lifetime's effort using the same critical term:

> All these bold fears
> Thou seest with peril I have answered;
> For all my reign hath been but as a scene
> Acting that argument.
> (*2 Henry IV*, IV.v.196–9)

We have seen earlier that Shakespeare thought a play had a *story*
to tell, but we should add that it might also have an *argument*. At
other times this is called the play's 'business', 'show', 'matter',
'substance', the 'force' of its story. These words identify the function

of an argument differently, but each implies that a play will *tell* or *show* its audience something that is inescapable, that it has an essential, undeniable, almost physical identity which can be described. This is different from local meanings that can be derived from any one moment of the drama, and different from a verbal statement appropriate to some particular context; the argument of a play is to be found in the continuous acting-out of all its scenes in prescribed order. In keeping with the idea of a 'cry of players' – the actors as a pack of hunting hounds – we might say that performance of any play is an activity in pursuit of some quarry which has to be caught in order to clinch or complete its story. The happenings on stage have a purpose to be fulfilled, an end to the hunt which makes its own mark and gives a sense of victory. An 'argument' in this sense would define one play over against another, even if they had the very same story, characters, and author.

We do not have Shakespeare's own use of the word to guide us, but we know that his Henry the Fourth would speak of the 'argument' of a play meaning a summing-up of what has been effected in it, like a judgement on a whole life-time that is made in retrospect and takes into account all that has happened. As a life leaves a finite inheritance – things that have been done, and cannot be undone – so a play leaves an indelible trace that by the end of a performance or reading should be plain for all to see. Accidental meanings and points of interest and controversy fall into place when viewed against this essential element of its design.

As used in Shakespeare's day, 'argument' did not necessarily imply a formal debate or wrangling. The verb 'to argue' implied 'to make clear, prove, assert', as well as 'to accuse or blame'. According to the *New English Dictionary*, Shakespeare's contemporaries took *argument* to mean some 'proof, evidence, manifestation, or token',[4] just as readily as a series of reasons in support of a point of view, a conflict of opinion, or a more formal debate. With regard to a play, its argument would be what its action makes clear, what it manifests, what evidence it gives for whatever debate or judgment may perhaps follow. It is something more substantial than its story as a sequence of events taking place on stage; it depends also on how those happenings are shown. In a word, it is what a play *does*.

For every play, Shakespeare made some very important and

distinctive decisions about the presentation of its story which shaped the experience it provides for an audience; together these decisions brought about the play's 'argument'. *Hamlet* need not have started on the battlements, the prince need not have had so many soliloquies, the players need not have been welcomed effusively or given opportunity to show a sample of their powers before performing *The Mousetrap*. The break-up of the players' performance need not have been followed by a series of short, rapid scenes, in which the king's life is spared, Polonius killed, and Hamlet captured and then banished; and these scenes need not have been interrupted with such a long meeting between Hamlet and his mother, briefly visited by his father's ghost. Ophelia's death need not have been reported by the queen; discussions between Claudius and Laertes need not have been so prolonged; the action need never have moved to a graveyard; the final scene did not have to include 'incensed' fighting. Hamlet's long absence from the stage could have been shortened; his return need not have been to an empty graveyard, but might have been sprung as a surprise in the middle of Ophelia's funeral or at court. Once we start suggesting other ways of presenting the story, Shakespeare's choices become more evident, together with his wilful shaping of the audience's experience. By no means can the reasons for his decisions be reconstructed, but his principal choices of what to enact on stage can be identified by an observer, and taken together they help to identify a very tangible argument in a play. This can then be used as a touchstone for all the meanings that arise accidentally when we examine the details of the text or when we read current criticism.

As we may be mistaken about a person's life until it is viewed as a whole, so meanings dependent on small details of a text may detain us solely because of their relevance to our own interests; it is the degree of their relevance to the main strategies of the play's presentation which helps us assess their limitations and the usefulness of our own perspective and perception. We might, of course, contend that a meaning which appears irrelevant to the play's argument comes from that part of Shakespeare's imagination that resisted his own conscious control and for that very reason should interest us most. Some critics do take this line, taking advantage of the openness of Shakespeare's writing and preferring their own intelligence to his, or their own vantage point at the end of the twentieth century. These critics would be able to

present the independence of their own discoveries more clearly
if they noted how far these stand outside what appears to be the
play's argument.

* * *

Space and time are major instruments in shaping the argument
of a play. Because the story of Hero and Claudio is only a part of
what is in hand and the narrative drive is therefore often slack,
Much Ado About Nothing shows more clearly than most plays how
an argument is independent of story and shaped according to
what action is presented on stage. The first scene takes time to
set up a pattern which will be repeated throughout. Leonato and
the ladies of his household are shown at home, hearing about
soldiers, talking about them, and then welcoming them formally;
and from within these two groupings, Beatrice, Benedick, Hero,
and Don John the Bastard, take more particular attention briefly.
But the larger part of the scene takes place after Leonato has left
the stage with Don Pedro, the chief guest: only two persons are
now on stage, Claudio, a young soldier and nobleman, and
Benedick, whom he has called back in order to talk privately about
Hero, Leonato's only daughter who has said not a word in his
presence, although others have talked and joked about her. Very
soon they are joined by Don Pedro who returns wanting to know
what they are talking about; Benedick is sent away and more
intimate confidences follow. The sequence of a stage crowded with
people in formal relationships giving way to an almost empty
stage with just a very few persons talking and being overheard
or questioned, will happen time and again in this comedy: it is a
recurring pattern in the activity on stage and provides the basic
shape of its argument.

The following scenes do not show the 'great supper' which is
prepared off-stage, the first of three feasts involved in the play's
story. Instead the audience hears yet more talk – about feasting,
betrothal, conspiracy, flirtation, disguise, youth and age. But the
earlier pattern is soon repeated when the stage becomes crowded
once more, with the formal beginnings of the masked dances which
follow the supper; then again the larger groups give way to much
smaller groups talking together. This celebration is also the first
of three 'night scenes', all to be marked by the carrying of torches

or other lights, and it is also the first of at least three scenes accompanied with music (if we assume that the bride will enter for the ceremony with the customary music). The argument of *Much Ado* is full of repeated patterns of action, so that scenes constantly reflect upon each other.

As its title gives warning[5] and the repeated patterns of action imply, the argument of this comedy is based in contrasts and comparisons. Part is concerned with talk, listening, eavesdropping, and a great deal of domestic business (including a scene of feminine intimacy rare in Shakespeare, when a young bride, alone with other women, prepares herself on the wedding morning). But all this is offset by the series of formal scenes which starts with the prince's arrival. Most notable of these is the wedding before a priest: here the stage fills without a word being spoken, but everyone moves in due order for the ceremony until, as in the first scene, these groupings break up for more private talk, desperately urgent and searching this time. Two formal scenes concern law and order; these show the setting of a watch and the conduct of a trial, and in both almost everything very quickly breaks up into ludicrous disorder. In Act V formality returns with a scene of mourning for Hero's supposed death, when music and torches dominate the stage-effects and arrest progress of the narrative. Then the masked ladies enter once more, ready for a reconvened wedding ceremony and this, after several hesitations and disturbances, brings the play to an end in the formality and liveliness of music and dance.

The argument of this play is an alternation of formalities which fill the stage, and private talk, conspiracy and eavesdropping when only a few people are on stage: it is much ado and it is almost nothing. A further patterning becomes evident in recurring night scenes: the first lightened by dance and laughter; the second made ominous, or at least 'deformed', by villainy, drink, and stupidity; the third, with music and torches, is both solemn and mysterious, though lightened by returning day:

> Good morrow, masters; put your torches out;
> The wolves have prey'd; and look, the gentle day,
> Before the wheels of Pheobus, round about
> Dapples the drowsy east with spots of grey.
>
> (V.iii.24–7)

Within the basic shape of alternate crowded and nearly empty stages, and recurrent darkness and light, music and silence, men and women do what they can to satisfy their desires. In their story a patient Friar Francis has some scheming influence, but its complications are resolved and the day is saved by the representatives of law and order – the clumsy, gullible, and self-important Dogberry and Verges. A further element is more lightly sketched in, although to sharp effect: Don John, against whom a military expedition had been launched, arrives in the first scene defeated and under house-arrest; he then sets a trap for Pedro and Claudio, takes pleasure in seeing its outcome, and then leaves the stage and the play, to be mentioned subsequently only in the last scene when the audience is told that he is recaptured and that 'brave punishments' will be devised for him after the marriage night.

Whatever interests arise from the dialogue, characters, and story of the play should be seen within these basic parameters of its argument – what the play does – even when they are most unconventional, such as a woman's desire to be a man, a man's to 'lock up all the gates of love', a constable's to 'be writ down an ass', a brother's to poison a brother, an old man's to fight a duel, a father's to have no child.[6] The basic argument provides the form in which all ideas are expressed, characters revealed, social customs exposed. But more than this, it also awakens and shapes the audience's most instinctive reactions by speaking directly to those senses of eye and ear which are common to all its members, irrespective of the extent to which the play's verbal ingenuity or passionate feeling may register individually. It is this argument which carries everything to a conclusion and marks the scope of all various meanings.

Exactly how argument serves to limit or define meanings could be demonstrated fairly only by considering a variety of suggested interpretations with as much care as they have been proposed, a task which cannot be tackled in part of a single chapter in a book about Shakespeare's writing for performance.[7] Perhaps the first consequence of considering this play's argument is the recognition that any single meaning should be related to a cyclic form of action which sets up wider perspectives in time and social circumstance than those encompassed by interpretations based on moments of crisis in the dialogue or on a single climactic conclusion.

Much Ado is rare among the comedies in that its argument is

contrived by contrasting behaviour but without moving the action from one place to another. More often a journey is under-
taken, as from Athens or some other city to the wood or forest,
from Venice to Belmont, from Orsino's palace to Olivia's house;
and by these journeys, the plays move from a comparatively ordinary reality to one more like a dream or the 'golden world' of
some other and fabulous time. When the play ends, a journey
back to the place of departure is about to begin, so that the basic
argument becomes very clear and carries with it a sense both of
awakening and of loss. This form of argument is varied from
comedy to comedy. In *The Merchant of Venice*, the perplexities of
the Venetian scenes come, at last, to be transferred to Belmont
and will remain there, in the place which had started as the
alternative world of the play. *Twelfth Night*'s argument is more
complicated, the location moving back and forth repeatedly between different kinds of reality: but talk of tempest and warfare
at sea, allusions to springtime in countryside and gardens, the
restless wit of a fool, together with incidental singing and music,
offer views of still other existences, all of which are intermittent
and most of which exist only in the mind. In *A Midsummer Night's
Dream*, the rehearsal and performance of *Pyramus and Thisbe* create their own kind of reality, which can move from the woods to
court, confident in its own powers and eventually holding everyone's attention for a time; one consequence is that the theatre
audience for this play becomes almost identical with another
audience on stage.

   To say that a play's argument is not so susceptible as its text
to personal interpretations and readings (or misreadings) is to
make a comparative judgement. There is, of course, more than
one way of describing a play's argument. The reason why all
such descriptions are more, and not less, reliable than interpretations based only and directly on quotation of the text is that they
focus on what is done, unquestionably, on stage and in a certain
sequence. If we fail to see some of the actions implied by the
text, or in some other way deduce incorrectly what should happen on stage, or if we fail to recognise recurring patterns or strange
anomalies, nevertheless the sum of everything that we do see will
express the substance of the play, which exists without the inter-
vention of wanton words; it will help us to be involved in the
whole play, rather than in one segment or strand of it. A description of its argument does not indicate what a play means or

put into words Shakespeare's intentions; but it does say something undeniable about the shape of the idea or ideas which informed its writing.

Even if we remain unsure of the argument of a play and unable to state it succinctly, an account of what happens physically on stage, in terms of entries and exits, groupings and regroupings, stage-business and prescribed behaviour, singing, dancing, eating, processing, chasing, hiding, fighting, and so forth, will lead an enquirer to that part of Shakespeare's invention that is literally and metaphorically substantial.

*   *   *

In the tragedies the stories are stronger and more easily defined than the multiple wooings and temporary confusions that are the staple of Shakespeare's comedies (at least until his last plays), but the killing of a king or the pursuit of revenge was not alone responsible for what one of these plays achieved. We have seen already how the plotting of speech and action, moment by moment, influenced character-presentation and the force, meaning, and implication of words spoken, and how it directed the audience's attention: all this mechanism and manipulation also helped to define a play's argument. (Plotting may be called the tactics of a play, story the occasion of its conflict, and argument its strategy.) Even a gripping and resonant story, such as that of *Othello*, *King Lear*, or *Macbeth*, will give less indication of what the play achieves for an audience than its argument, which is how Shakespeare chose to present the story and so shape the substance of the drama. The most efficient way of summing up the effect of a tragedy is to consider which elements of the story Shakespeare has shown on stage and how he has done so. In relation to this argument, the *effect* of the story can be assessed and the relevance of all verbally specific meanings adjudicated.

The story of *Othello* is presented, like those in several of the comedies, by moving the action from one place to another, from Venice to Cyprus; but here several distinct locations are used in each place so that they give an alternation of private and public incidents, and gradually, in the second location, the private ones provide the more sustained scenes, and this tragedy, exceptionally for Shakespeare, ends in the bedroom. Urgent and violent incidents keep recurring, almost none of them to be found in the story of the source: the arousal of Brabantio's household after Desdemona's elopement, the encounter with Othello's armed guard, the messengers bringing news of a national emergency, the drunken mutiny which 'frights the isle From her propriety' (II.iii.167–8), Othello's fit, which leaves him senseless, his public humiliation of his wife, the killing of Roderigo and wounding of Cassio, and the deaths of the very last scene, one painfully slow and the others violent and sudden.

Also remarkable and used to unusual effect is a series of incidents which are said to happen off-stage or at some other time: the continuing threat of war from the Turks; the storm at sea which separates the ships bearing Othello and Desdemona to Cyprus; the 'disastrous chances' and battles, and the encounters with Cannibals and Anthropophagi, which Othello had talked about as he wooed Desdemona (I.iii.129–46); the two-hundred-year-old Sybil who had embroidered the fatal handkerchief which Desdemona loses, and the deaths of all the virgins whose hearts provided dye for the embroidery's silk (III.iv.69–75); the madness of Barbary, the maid of Desdemona's mother, who 'was in love' and 'died singing' (IV.iii.25–32); the 'base Indian' (or Judean) who 'threw a pearl away' and the Turk who was taken 'by th'throat' and killed (V.ii.350–1, 355–9). All these are additions to the story which was Shakespeare's source and are not presented on stage; but what *is* shown there repeatedly and with shocking clarity is the effect on the characters of these off-stage happenings, some of them distant in time or too fabulous to warrant total belief. They are mentioned briefly, but their effect in the thoughts, speech, and passions of the protagonists are of crucial importance. Merely the mention of them changes tone, tempo, and focus, and helps to delineate the emotional and mental forces at work in the tragedy: so they, too, influence what the play does, the shape of its argument.

Throughout, Iago manipulates others and, until he has made Othello believe his wife is false to him, he is the one character who addresses the audience directly in sustained soliloquy. Towards the end, however, he, with all the main characters, seems helpless as the story draws to a conclusion in a way that none of them could entirely foresee and none can prevent: so fate seems to take a hand in events, and, more certainly, so do those dangerous deceits which burn like 'mines of sulphur' within a jealous man (III.iii.330–3). The manners of the deaths show personal resources that also could scarcely be foreseen: Emilia's selfless courage; Othello's renewed tenderness as he kisses his sleeping wife, and his perfectly executed and surprise suicide before bending down to kiss her dead body; Desdemona's return to consciousness and her lie to protect her husband; and Iago's silence. All this is present in ways that grab a stunned attention, so that repercussions in the minds of the audience, on stage and in the auditorium, take time to register fully.

On occasion during the earlier parts of the play, fluent speeches almost monopolise attention, words outriding action, but some further knowledge and feelings are also present in the consciousness of its leading characters, although almost entirely hidden. This interior world is fully expressed only in the last act when, under great pressure of events, minds are prised open or speakers need to make themselves fully known. This does not mean that attention is finally drawn only to personal predicaments and relationships: in the persons of Lodovico and his train, Venice is brought back to the stage for the last scene, and in the minds of the leading characters, as they are revealed at last, race, time, heaven and hell, affairs of the state, and responsibility to others are among the dominant concerns.

For Shakespeare's major plays, simple descriptions and standard categories will not serve to describe all that is made evident on stage in a particular order. For each text a new form of argument seems to have been invented. For several plays it may be said to take the form of a journey, but even this pattern changes. So in *King Lear*, while the location of its action moves from one dwelling to another, and then to the Heath, Dover Beach and the final battle-field, its plotting does not emphasise the king's travelling but rather the successive meetings which this involves. First he journeys to visit his daughters; then, going out onto the Heath, he has a closer encounter than before with his Fool, until this companion drops out of the action and his place is taken by Edgar, whom Lear meets as a frenzied and naked madman, pursued by fiends and studying how to 'kill vermin' (III.iv.155). When the supposedly mad Poor Tom announces that he smells 'the blood of a British man' (III.iv.180), he and Lear become so close in feeling that they leave the stage together. When he is next seen, Lear's meetings have become imaginary, as he starts to arraign his daughters, sensing their nightmarish presence amid the barking of dogs. That done, he is led off stage to sleep, only to reappear to meet the suffering and blinded Gloucester: Lear does not know to whom he speaks, but at once pardons the helpless man, whom he assumes to have committed adultery. This encounter starts by questioning all appearances of authority and justice, but when the king recognises Gloucester and so meets someone from his earlier life, he changes rapidly, at first to 'preach' patience and then to exact cruel punishment like that he had heard in the thunder and in the ravings of Poor Tom:

> And when I have stol'n upon these son-in-laws,
> Then kill, kill, kill, kill, kill, kill!
>
> (IV.vi.187–8)

Seeing Cordelia's soldiers, he assumes that they come to capture him. But they offer respect and he is, for a moment, conscious of his own royalty; then he rushes off as if thinking himself a hunted creature of the wild. Lear's next encounter is after he has been brought to Cordelia and given every possible attention: the meeting between them is full of new tenderness and simplicity. Whatever happens, even defeat in battle, he will not be parted from the one daughter he can trust and who forgives him:

> He that parts us shall bring a brand from heaven
> And fire us hence like foxes.
>
> (V.iii.22–3)

This sequence of meetings does not end off-stage with the assassination of Cordelia and his instinctive killing of her assailant. With his daughter dead in his arms, he comes back onto the stage to confront the 'men of stones' whom he had at one time ruled. Recognition of the faithful Kent, who had served him in disguise, makes little impression. Lear's last efforts are an attempt to get everyone on stage to see that there is breath on Cordelia's lips – a sign of life that possibly he believes he can see: here he seems to be more dependent on others than ever before.

Edgar, Albany, and Kent are only intermittently in focus at the conclusion of the play and yet they are all vital parts of its argument, having been given sustained and independent emphasis during the course of the story. Supporting characters have an especially large role in *King Lear*, the only tragedy to be given a fully developed subplot. The story of the Earl of Gloucester and his two sons, with the relationship of one to Lear and of the other to Lear's daughters Goneril and Regan, provides a complex web of action that is presented in a number of dramatic modes, ranging from the social comedy of an old father and a clever son, to the sensational intrigue of revenge driven by lust and ambition. So strongly does this subplot develop that Shakespeare may have had Gloucester die off-stage in order that attention is centred on Lear in the last episodes of the play without too much distraction. The presentation of the Earl of Kent almost amounts to a third subplot concerned with service and mastery; besides scenes with the king and all three daughters, Shakespeare provided incidents in which Kent pits himself against Oswald, who is a young ambitious servant intimate with Goneril and then with Regan.

The play's argument has both uncommon width and intense concentration: the journeys of both Gloucester and Lear provide a series of very varied and fully stated conflicts and a number of more private moments of reconciliation. Any attempt at a criticism of the tragedy should take account of the sequence, shape, and substance of this argument. This does not involve simplification or make criticism suddenly much easier: rather it would shift the ground of all enquiry to what is done on stage over the length of a performance. In other words, criticism would be brought into relationship with what is the most basic of all tasks in writing for performance.

*   *   *

Shakespeare's plays have both an argument and numerous meanings. Some arguments positively encourage readers and audiences to come to their own decisions about meaning. This can be achieved by the way a story is staged and also by not staging certain episodes found in the source. For example, two scenes in the first Act of *Richard II* set Bolingbroke and Mowbray accusing each other of high treason as if in a court of law. They are indeed in the presence of their king as charges are made at some length, but these are not simple denunciations, because both of them refer to Richard, hinting at his complicity in the death of Woodstock: all three, including the king, sitting for much of the time in silence, will keep wary eyes on the others. But the issue remains unresolved, to be a continuing spur for the audience's questions. Richard is

subsequently accused of living riotously in expensive self-indul-
gence, but nowhere does the play show this happening. Bolingbroke
will later condemn the king's favourites to death for corruption
and illegality, and implies that their master had approved of what
they had done:

> You have in manner with your sinful hours
> Made a divorce betwixt his queen and him;
> Broke the possession of a royal bed,
> And stain'd the beauty of a fair queen's cheeks
> With tears drawn from her eyes by your foul wrongs.
>   (III.i.11–5)

But nothing of this is seen or heard on stage. On the contrary the
queen is shown being comforted by Richard's favourites, and her
wishes seem to be bound up with her husband's well-being; she
weeps for his absence and the danger he is in, not for the break-
up of their marriage. Richard is also condemned for ordering crown
lands to be leased out and for confiscating his banished cousin's
estates to finance a war in Ireland; but no alternative measures
are suggested, which is strange unless we are to assume that the
king should sit still in England while rebels rob and pillage what
everyone assumes to be his country's lands.

In many ways the audience is invited to make judgements on
the king and then is not given grounds for doing so. Richard's
uncles and elder statesmen are sure they know how he should
rule and tell him so on every possible occasion; but they prove
unable to control their own sons or manage their own affairs with
much efficiency. Richard might have justified his autocratic decisions as a means of gathering money in hard times, and his main-
tenance of a 'great' court as the way to ensure loyalty by 'liberal
largesse' – very much as Elizabeth I did when faced with inflation
and the opposition of the established nobility and newly assertive
commons – but he does not bother to do so. The presentation of the
story of *Richard II*, from beginning to end, raises a series of questions about political prudence and decision-making, about rights,
authority, experience, economics and taxation, religion, and history;
and it does this in so open-ended a manner that an audience is
bound to take sides variously and speculate on whether the actors
are performing the text as its author intended. The argument in this
play instigates and supports an ongoing debate about meaning.

*   *   *

Some critics believe that Shakespeare was a writer for all occasions and all opinions, rather like Feste who claims he is 'for all waters' when he has succeeded in putting on a new disguise (IV.ii.61). But the many meanings that are found in the plays are not evidence that the dramatist had no ideas that he cared about or none that he wished to show at work in his plays. Shakespeare's most sustained and imaginative thinking is not easily reduced to prose definitions or suggestions. His thinking discovered itself in the task of shaping the plays as complete works written for performance, in all the variety of implication and possible realisation that theatrical performance implies. If we try to understand the arguments of the plays we will be trying to understand the shaping of entire plays for performance, and that is to come as close as possible to understanding the shaping powers of ideas about men and women, and about society, politics, history, philosophy, and all kinds of belief – closer than when we concentrate on any of the verbally specific and immediately exciting meanings that arise from details of texts.

Acknowledgements

I am most grateful to colleagues and members of my seminars at the University of Michigan for stimulus and encouragement during the last seven or eight years when I was writing this book. I am also glad to acknowledge financial help from the university's Office of the Vice President for Research, the Horace H. Rackham School of Graduate Studies, the International Institute, the School of Music, and the Department of Theatre and Drama. I also owe a great debt to colleagues in other universities, to the many theatre productions I have seen, and, still more, to the actors and everyone else involved in the plays I have directed in England and in North America.

I have tried to benefit from careful comments on the first draft of this book which were made for me by Anthony Thorlby and Keirnan Ryan, the former a true friend and counsellor over many years, the latter a valued and honest critic. I am most grateful for the attention they have given my book, which is I hope the better for the trouble they have taken. Its defects are, of course, my own and not theirs.

At the publisher, Margaret Bartley has been an understanding and most supportive editor, and Valery Rose and her colleagues at Longworth have been most expert and timely: for all this help I give my warmest thanks.

JOHN RUSSELL BROWN

Notes

Note to the Introduction

1. I have written about some of these experiences in 'Jatra Theatre and Elizabethan Dramaturgy', *New Theatre Quarterly*, x: 40 (1994), 331–47; and 'Back to Bali', in *The Critical Gamut*, ed. Enoch Brater (Ann Arbor, Mich.: University of Michigan Press, forthcoming). See also my 'Foreign Shakespeare and English-speaking Audiences', in *Foreign Shakespeare: Contemporary Performance*, ed. Dennis Kennedy (Cambridge: Cambridge University Press, 1993) pp. 21–35.

Notes to Chapter 1: Theatre

1. Interview with Tony Coult, *Plays and Players*, December 1975.
2. 'Introduction: "The Rational Theatre"', *Plays: Two* (London: Methuen, 1978) p. xiv.
3. Interview with Albert Hunt, *Arena* Theatre Special, *Playwrights of the Seventies*, BBC2 TV, 15 June 1977.
4. Interview with Duff Newton, *The Theatre Today*, BBC Radio, 22 April 1959.
5. Interview with Helen Palmer, *Today Programme*, BBC Radio, 1 March 1979.
6. Interview with Michael Billington, *Tonight*, BBC2, 29 June 1979.
7. Quoted from an article by Samuel G. Freedman, 'The Blue-Collar Eloquence of David Mamet', *New York Times Magazine*, 21 April 1985.
8. *1 Henry VI*, III.ii.41.
9. *Romeo and Juliet*, Second Quarto, I.v.1.
10. *Julius Caesar*, IV.i.68.
11. Folio text, V.i.1.
12. *Timon*, III.iv.1.
13. *Coriolanus*, III.ii.106.
14. *Tempest*, III.iii.83.
15. See John Marston, *Antonio and Mellida*, II.i.21.
16. *Everywoman in Her Humour* (Anon., 1607–8); ed. A. H. Bullen (1885), p. 354.
17. *Troilus and Cressida*, I.iii.156.
18. *Henry V*, Prol., 4; *Macbeth*, I.iii.128.
19. See M. C. Bradbrook, *The Rise of the Common Player* (London: Chatto, 1962) passim.
20. Jean Genet, *Reflections on the Theatre and Other Writings*, tr. Richard Seaver (London: Faber, 1972) pp. 40–1.

21. Ibid., p. 31.
22. Letter to Paule Thévenen (24 February 1948), as quoted by Martin Esslin in his own translation, in *Artaud* (London: Fontana, Collins, 1976) pp. 89–90.

Notes to Chapter 2: Words

1. See *1 Henry VI*, III.iii.40–58; *2 Henry VI*, I.i.151–6; *3 Henry VI*, III.ii.150 and III.iii.112; and *Titus*, V.iii.85.
2. *1 Henry VI*, I.i.77.
3. *John*, III.i.63 and II.i.582.
4. *Richard III*, I.ii.168, III.i.13 and IV.i.79–80.
5. *Titus*, IV.iv.90.
6. *Love's Labour's Lost*, V.ii.741.
7. Ibid., II.i.73 and 76, I.i.170 and 176, V.i.13, 80–1 and 33.
8. *Love's Labour's Lost*, V.i.128–9.
9. *Much Ado About Nothing*, II.i.98 and 103; and see ll. 109, 111 and 117.
10. See *Merry Wives*, I.i.95 and 187, I.iii.14, I.iv.74–5 and 93, II.ii.14 and 36, III.i.72, and III.iv.29.
11. See J. Marston, *The Scourge of Villany* (1598), Sat. x; and *The Return from Parnassus, Part II* (?1599), III.i.
12. See *2 Henry VI*, III.iii.25; and *Lear*, V.iii.313.
13. *Much Ado*, IV.i.155–70.
14. Perhaps Shakespeare was glancing back in his own mind to what the words of Shylock's 'bond' did not 'expressly' say; see *The Merchant of Venice*, IV.i.300ff.
15. *Hamlet*, II.ii.248–9 and II.i.66.
16. Ibid., II.ii.581 and V.i.274–8, 278–9.
17. Ibid., V.i.292 and III.i.75.
18. *1 Henry IV*, V.i.129–39; and *2 Henry IV*, II.i.107–8.
19. *Hamlet*, II.ii.581.
20. Ibid., III.ii.136–7.
21. Ibid., III.iii.97.

Notes to Chapter 3: Speech and Action

1. 'Address to the Students of the University of Harvard, March 30, 1885: The Art of Acting', *The Drama* (London: Heinemann, 1893) p. 51.
2. Interview, *Observer* (London), 9 February 1969.
3. *Stage Directions* (New York: Random House, 1963) p. 5
4. Ibid., p. 4.
5. Ibid., p. 7.
6. Interview, *Observer* (London), 19 October 1975.

7. Discussion recorded in John Barton, *Playing Shakespeare* (London and New York: Methuen, 1985) p. 209.
8. Georges Banu, 'Peter Brook's Six Days', *New Theatre Quarterly*, III: 10 (1987) p. 104.
9. *Players of Shakespeare: Essays in Shakespearean Performance by Twelve Players with the Royal Shakespeare Company*, ed. Philip Brockbank (Cambridge: Cambridge University Press, 1985) p. 43.
10. *Sunday Times* (London), 24 April 1966.
11. *Macbeth*, I.iv.11–12; and *Lear*, I.i.296–7.
12. Richard Flecknoe, *A Short Discourse of the English Stage* (London, 1664); quoted in E. K. Chambers, *The Elizabethan Stage* (Oxford: Oxford University Press, 1923) vol. IV, p. 370.
13. The short passage in Holinshed's *Chronicles* which was Shakespeare's main source for this scene records that the king was told of 'great forces which the Duke of Lancaster had got together against him' and that these rebels 'would rather die than give place, as well for the hatred as fear which they had conceived at him'.

Notes to Chapter 4: Characters

1. *Much Ado About Nothing*, II.i.275–6.
2. *Richard II*, v.v.49.
3. *Othello*, v.ii.347; *Lear* III.ii.60; and *Hamlet*, II.ii.565 and v.ii.222–4.
4. *Much Ado About Nothing*, v.ii.63.
5. *Players of Shakespeare*, ed. Philip Brockbank (Cambridge: Cambridge University Press, 1985) p. 161.
6. Ibid.
7. *2 Henry IV*, I.ii.149–50.
8. *Romeo and Juliet*, II.iv.25–6.
9. Tennessee Williams, *Where I Live: Selected Essays*, ed. Christine R. Day and Bob Woods (New York: New Directions, 1978) pp. 157–8.

Notes to Chapter 5: Interplay

1. Quoted in Margaret Croyden, 'Behind the Masks, Violent Sensuality', *New York Times*, 16 November 1971.
2. For example, see Maynard Mack's comment, pp. 42–3 above.
3. *Twelfth Night*, I.v.234.
4. Ibid., II.iii.137ff.
5. Ibid., v.i.364.
6. *Love's Labour's Lost*, v.ii.871–2.
7. *2 Henry IV*, v.v.85–91.
8. Ibid., II.iv.178–9.
9. See *Othello*, v.ii.132.
10. *Hamlet*, III.ii.354ff.

11. *Lear*, I.ii.12.
12. *Hamlet*, II.ii.122.
13. Ibid., I.iii.99–100.
14. *Much Ado*, IV.i.287.
15. *Antony and Cleopatra*, I.i.47, 48.

Notes to Chapter 6: Openness

1. *Some Unconscious Influences in the Theatre* (Cambridge: Cambridge University Press, 1967) pp. 7–10.
2. See 'Writing for Myself', *Twentieth Century*, CLXIX (1961), 174.
3. Interview, *New Theatre Quarterly*, III: 10 (1987), 158.
4. 'Drama and Dialectics of Violence' (an interview), *Theatre Quarterly*, II: 5 (1972), 12.
5. *Peter Hall's Diaries* (London: Hamilton, 1983) pp. 465, 467.
6. *Julius Caesar*, I.ii.227–60; *Measure for Measure*, I.i.69–71; *Henry VIII*, V.iv.57–8.
7. *A Midsummer Night's Dream*, V.i.90–105.
8. *Twelfth Night*, V.i.394; *As You Like It*, Epilogue; *All's Well*, Epilogue.
9. See the Quarto's opening stage-direction at I.ii.
10. *Hamlet*, II.ii.600–1.
11. Ibid., I.iv.89–90.
12. Ibid., V.ii.293.
13. Ibid., III.ii.136–7.
14. Ibid., III.i.75.
15. Ibid., V.ii.387–92.
16. See pp. 77–82 above.
17. *Richard II*, II.ii; see pp. 46–53 above.
18. *My Life in Art*, trans. J. J. Robins (New York: Theatre Arts Books 1948) p. 78.
19. Interview in the *Guardian*, 10 March 1982.

Notes to Chapter 7: Happenings

1. *A Midsummer Night's Dream*, I.ii.10–11 and V.i.56–7; *Hamlet*, II.ii.392–5.
2. *Henslowe's Diary*, ed. R. A. Foakes and R. T. Rickert (Cambridge: Cambridge University Press, 1961) p. 85.
3. But see *Titus Andronicus*, III.i.134, where in opposition to presenting 'dumb shows', 'Plot some device' may refer to writing a stage show.
4. *Richard III*, ed. Anthony Hammond, Arden Shakespeare (London: Methuen, 1981) p. 73. The following account of the sources of the play is indebted to this and other recent editions.
5. See pp. 104–5 above.
6. Hotspur, in his fight with Hal, also dies in the middle of a sentence; see *1 Henry IV*, V.iv.86.

Notes to Chapter 8: Meanings and Arguments

1. As one example of how opinions on the same text differ (where very many could be quoted), Valerie Traub's *Desire and Anxiety: Circulations of Sexuality in Shakespearean Drama* (London: Routledge, 1992) cites three notions besides her own of Rosalind's role in *As You Like It* and explains why they differ:

   > The distance traversed in the progression from [C. L.] Barber to [Louis Adrian] Montrose to [Jean] Howard indicates a corresponding movement from an essentialist view of gender, to an emphasis on social structure as determining gender, to an assertion of the limited possibilities of subversive manipulation within dominant cultural codes. (pp. 123–4)

2. *Quaestiones quodlibetales*, ed. P. Mandonnet (Paris, 1926), vii, 14, p. 275, as quoted, for example, in E. H. Gombrich, *Symbolic Images: Studies in the Art of the Renaissance* (3rd edn, 1985) p. 16.
3. See Inge Leimberg, '"Golden Apollo, a poor humble swain . . .": a study of names in *The Winter's Tale*', *Shakespeare Jahrbuch West* (1991), 136–58.
4. See, for example, *Twelfth Night*, III.ii.12: 'This was a great argument of love in her toward you.'
5. There is a pun on *nothing* and *noting*.
6. See *Much Ado*, IV.i.299 and 303; IV.ii.70–80; I.iii.62; V.i.80–5; and IV.i.123–9.
7. A beginning can be made by noting very briefly some discordant accounts of the comedy. J. R. Mulryne suggested that it offered an experience 'of "pleasurable reassurance" – a demonstration in terms of theatre that good will conquer, that "all shall be well"': this notion that some good is finally triumphant runs counter to the cyclic nature of the argument. Paul and Miriam Mueschke argued that its theme 'is honor, that its spirit is less joyous than reflective, and that courtship, a peripheral concern, is presented as an imminent threat to masculine honor': this captures the 'reflective' nature of the argument, but the privileging of honour as a theme undervalues the domesticity and stupidity which are also part of what is 'made evident' in the comedy. Barbara Everett saw the comedy at one with others of Shakespeare's in that 'some more important things take the place of what is lost, all perhaps developing out of the sense of that loss; a wisdom, balance, and generosity of mind and feeling, largely expressed through the women's roles': this reading places more weight on fleeting impressions in the concluding scene than the recurrent nature of the play's activity can support. Carol Cook counters these critics by arguing that 'the play masks, as well as exposes, the mechanisms of masculine power and that, insofar as it avoids what is crucial to its conflicts, the explicitly offered comic resolution is something of an artful dodge': this again privileges the last moment, while noting the recurrent nature of much of the action.

See J. R. Mulryne, *Shakespeare: 'Much Ado About Nothing'* (London: Arnold, 1965), especially pp. 14–25; Paul and Miriam Mueschke, 'Illusion and Metamorphosis in *Much Ado About Nothing*', *Shakespeare Quarterly*, xviii (1967) pp. 53–67; Barbara Everett, 'Something of Great Constancy', *Critical Quarterly*, iii (1961), 319–35; and Carol Cook, '"The Sign and Semblance of Her Honor": Reading Gender Difference in *Much Ado About Nothing*, PMLA, CI.ii (1986) 187.

Index